After Dinner Conversation

Philosophy | Ethics Short Story Magazine

March 2025

After Dinner Conversation Magazine – March 2025

This magazine publishes fictional stories that explore ethical and philosophical questions in an informal manner. The purpose of these stories is to generate thoughtful discussion in an open and easily accessible manner.

Names, characters, businesses, organizations, places, events, and incidents are either the product of the author's imagination or are used fictitiously. Any resemblance to actual persons, living or dead, events, or locales is entirely coincidental. The magazine is published monthly in print and electronic format.

Vol. 6, No. 3

Copyright © 2025 After Dinner Conversation ™
Editor in Chief: *Kolby Granville*
Story Editor: *R.K.H. Ndong*
Copy Editors: *Stephen Repsys & Kate Bocassi*
Cover Design: *Shawn Winchester*
Design, layout, and discussion questions by After Dinner Conversation.

https://www.afterdinnerconversation.com

After Dinner Conversation is an independent nonprofit publisher. We believe in fostering meaningful discussions among friends, family, and students to enhance humanity through truth-seeking, reflection, and respectful debate. To achieve this, we publish philosophical and ethical short story fiction accompanied by discussion questions.

Table Of Contents

* * *

From the Editor

Can I just *rant* for a minute? My rant is this: *read primary source material*!

You want to call someone a communist? First, read *The Communist Manifesto*. You want to call them a Nazi? Have you read *Mein Kampf*? You want to tell someone what American democracy means? Have you read *The Federalist Papers*? Have you read *The Wealth of Nations*?

Have you read the *actual opinion* of *Roe v. Wade*, or *Loving v. Virginia*, or *Brown v. Board of Education*, or *Obergefell v. Hodges*? Have you read the Bible and the Koran? Have you read *Uncle Tom's Cabin* or *Narrative of the Life of Frederick Douglass* or *The Interesting Narrative of the Life of Olaudah Equiano*? Then how can you possible discuss chattel slavery?

I could go on, but you get the point. If you haven't read the *primary source*, when you argue about these topics, you aren't arguing about what these documents say, you are arguing about *what you have been told they say*!

No, you don't have to read every primary source document in the world. But pick five, or ten, as a starting point. Heck, listen to the audiobook in your car! Then, when someone tells you what a document says, you will know if they are telling you what it *actually* says...

Stepping off my soap box now. And yes, I have strong feelings about the education system too...

Kolby Granville – Editor

The Apath

A.J. Parker

* * *

Content Disclosure: Sexual Situations; Depiction of Drug Use; Substance Addiction Themes; Strong Language

* * *

The line to buy Happiness was long.

Finn walked past expectant guests waiting to get into the sharp, white building. A procession of people curled around the corner, hair glinting like plastic, skin as smooth as rubber. Marcus's Delights sold only the best emotions. Everyone knew that. The storefront was all glass, so it could boast of its fluttery, color-changing light. Crystal vials sparkled on purple cushions, and the edible items on display were fresh out of the oven. Even the pills were put in dainty little bottles, rubbed spotless to be chic enough for uptown folk. The product was kept in locked glass cases like fine jewelry.

Finn continued down the street until his feet transitioned to cobbled sidewalk. He knew he was close to Mammy's when the buildings around him grew rickety and gray, and the sky was striped with animated billboards and electric wires.

"Out to run errands, Finn?" Elephant, the security guard, asked from his ripped barstool. His accent was an oscillating blend of Irish and British. He was all shoulders, torso, and arms, beefier than any man Finn had seen. Elephant was a staple at Mammy's, more decoration than anything else. An electrified, holographic gate to a darkened staircase was the real barrier to entry.

"Only for your best," Finn said, to which Elephant gave a hearty laugh and replied, "Not that you could afford it."

"Careful there, or I might go to Harry's instead."

"Ho ho ho," Elephant said. "Somebody call True Designs."

"Why? They're already listening."

"That's enough of that. Go on in, boy."

Elephant waved a palm over a keypad, and the gate retracted. This was always Finn's favorite part—walking the roughened stairs. There was nothing but possibility there as the distance shortened between him and what he wanted to feel. There were no lines or diligent security cameras, no boasting glass-front windows. Who knew what he was going to get? As he climbed the scuffed steps, it was just him, the dying lightbulb above, and the peeling charcoal walls.

When he entered, his least favorite employee was working the register. Mariana was a fixture at Mammy's, too, but not a decoration. Her hair was a ruffled white and gray, which complemented her beady brown eyes. She wore a permanent frown. It was just the two of them inside the store. He nodded to her respectfully, but she ignored him as she sorted a jar full of Mixed Emotion lollipops.

Mammy's didn't put their product on display like

Marcus's Delights. At Mammy's, vials upon vials dotted the walls, gripped by a claw, each labeled respectively. There was no organization to it, no luxury to it. He skimmed the wall—neon green for Jealousy, gray for Nervousness, amethyst for Awareness, orange for Frustration. He was surprised they hadn't been shut down by the National Health Service yet, but as long as Mammy's kept their "True Designs merchandise sold here" sign up in the window, their asses were covered. Even if that merchandise was only candy.

Old felt jewelry holders decorated the dinged-up tables in the middle of the room. Tiny baggies squeezed into the place earrings would go. Individually bubble-wrapped pills filled the sunken necklace compartments. Flavored candies sat in the ring holders. It seemed laughable compared to Marcus's. Finn picked up a small bag of Distraction before carrying on.

He found himself in front of the wall again. Yellow for Panic. Crimson for Vengeance. Fuchsia for Enthusiasm. You wouldn't find any Happiness there. It was a secondhand shop full of cheap knockoffs and watered-down products.

Who would buy the bad emotions? That was the public debate, at first. The answer was simple. The ones who couldn't afford any better.

Finn hovered in front of a swirling blue and gray vial. He checked the price tag.

"Ten pounds sterling," the cashier said, startling him. "Knocked down the price. It's just been sitting there, collecting dust."

He picked it off the wall. When he was done perusing the store, he set his collection of items onto the checkout counter.

"Would that be all?"

"And one of those." He pointed to the lollipops in front of the register. She added it to his purchase. He paid with his wrist chip and then dug a hand into the candy jar. He peeled the wrapper off. Her eyes widened as he placed the lollipop into his mouth, crunching the wrapper in his fist.

"Didn't you want to check what you got?"

"Thanks." He took his bag and left.

When he was outside, far out of Elephant's sight, he uncrumpled the wrapper. The groovy pink lettering on the foil read "Desire."

He gave a dry laugh and kept sucking.

* * *

Sarah didn't say no when he invited her over. They did lines of her leftover Intrigue.

"Do you feel it?" she asked as they sat on the sagging brown couch. His apartment's yellowing walls shimmered. He could see the individual nicks the place had collected over the years, thin lines on the floor from dragged furniture and scuffed corners from negligence.

"Yeah," he said, though his pupils were already dilated.

"Yeah?" she asked again.

"Yeah."

He kissed her first because he knew women liked that. Everything about her was vibrant. The blond at the base of her mascaraed eyelashes. The stained pink bra she wore, peeking out from behind her tank top. He squished her skin between his fingers, feeling peach fuzz. She was a marvel of mediocrity. He dug his fingers into the outside of her thighs and worked his hands up her supple body. She groaned. It was guttural and ugly. He took her chin in both his hands.

"What are you doing?" she asked as he titled her head side to side.

"I just wanted to get a good look at you."

She blushed as he examined the unkempt hairs around her eyebrows and the faded tattoo on her collarbone. Her roots were dark from poor maintenance, and her rosy lipstick had been smudged. He pinned her shoulder down against the couch where she sat, freeing his other hand, as his lips found her neck. She tilted her head back and closed her eyes, moaning.

She was interesting, wasn't she?

* * *

"It's no fun anymore, is it?" Finn waved the smoke away, the artificial tobacco leaving a burnt taste in his mouth. His friend's kitchen was crowded with partygoers, most of whom had become onlookers to Finn's monologue. Music pulsed in the background. Sarah giggled as he pointed at her with the cigarette between his long fingers. "They keep us alive longer so they can sell us more things. We used to just die, you know."

He had tried a real cigarette only once (he was mates with an antiques collector), but it wasn't hard to figure out why they had been discontinued. The curl of poisoned tobacco was addictive, the taste terribly good. This imitation was just a mouthfeel: thick, flavored water vapor and a smokey taste. Unregulated feelings were the only dangerous thing left in the world.

Sarah opened her mouth and waited, her pink tongue on display. He popped the cigarette in as he leaned against the fridge, one leg propped up.

"Wouldn't you rather be alive?" she asked, mouth full. She blew smoke directly into Finn's face and giggled again. He watched her tongue play with the end of the cigarette.

Finn liked Sarah. He liked her thick Northern accent and her crispy yellow hair. He liked her uneven teeth. She was the furthest you could get from the plastic sheen of the New Designs uptown who sold out for new hair and new skin and new teeth. Sarah wasn't very smart, but that's what he liked best about her.

"Bloody hell," Freud interrupted. "I shouldn't have given you that Energy shot when you came in."

"You know what counters Energy?" Xi said as he lounged against the back doorframe. His shock of black hair was impeccably clean and his beige skin, impeccably smooth. Cool air wafted in through the screen door. Finn took his cigarette back and grinned, leaving the smoke in Sarah's mouth behind.

The screen door creaked shut as they transitioned to the overcrowded townhome's porch. Xi looked clean in silver pants and a matching silver overcoat. Underneath it, he wore the black button-up all the coders were required to wear to the office. It was the best way to differentiate bot from person. Xi could afford to live uptown—he had access to the best products because of it.

"You've taken this before, right?" Xi asked as they sat on the back porch. Moths buzzed at the light above them. The yard was tiny, squishing them between the hot water unit and the trash cans. Though it was significantly quieter outside, the neighbors were used to Freud's rowdiness by now.

"Yes," Finn lied.

Xi took out the small vial. When he unscrewed the lid, a dropper came out. "Let's see what a wee bit of Calm can do for you."

"Couldn't shell out for the proper stuff? Tranquility,

Serenity, Bullshitery?"

"Now that's above my pay grade. Cheers."

Xi twisted his mouth, head leaning back, as he put the drops into his eyes. Xi passed it to Finn, who followed suit. He sniffed when he sat up, blinking the clear liquid away. It stung at first, but nothing Finn wasn't used to. That's how you knew it was real and not the diluted kind they sold at Mammy's.

Xi stared at the sky. It was one of those nights where the constellations were blinking in and out sporadically. Someone would have to call maintenance to reprogram the drones. Xi snorted and shook his head.

"All that taxpayer money and they can't even get the fucking stars to work."

"Let the Design girls worry about it. They're the ones who believe in that shit." Finn passed the cigarette to Xi, letting out smoke. All he could think about was what it was missing.

"I'm sure you dream of getting one of those New Design girls underneath you, eh?"

"Never."

"Never?

"There's something unnatural about them, isn't there?"

"And this is natural?" Xi asked, waving the fake cigarette around.

"It's affordable," Finn said. He took the vial from where it sat on the steps next to them.

"You know not to take too much, right?"

"I'm not a dumbass."

It had been plastered up on flashing billboards and portable screens his whole life. "Get emotional. On occasion." The pretty model would smile, teeth too white, as she held out a bright yellow tab in her palm. She swallowed it with as little thought as she would a painkiller, and afterward, put her thumb up, laughing as she said, "It's *occasionally* good!"

They even named their parent company "The Occasion Corporation," as if that covered their asses when the lawsuits trickled in. They had created a feat of science. A way to heighten emotions. A way to maintain them. The warning labels weren't big enough, so they made them bigger. The more of an emotion you took, the less of it you could feel on your own later. Their lawyers made a fortune, but once the product was out there, it couldn't be taken back, only regulated.

Finn didn't mind. He didn't have a lot of use for Calm in his life. He put two more splashes in each eye. When he blinked his vision clear, everything in front of him was smooth and pastel. It wasn't black outside; it was a dark cerulean. He looked at his hands. They gleamed like he had moisturized them. Everything was slow and syrupy. Peaceful. He liked the way the stairs creaked as he shuffled his weight and how Xi's jacket shimmered underneath the fuzzy light.

"Finnnn," Sarah drawled as she cracked open the screen door. "Are you having fun without me?"

She came down to him and when she sat, she sat in his lap, wrapping her legs around him. Her tights rippled as her dress rode up.

"That's my cue," Xi said, slipping the vial into his pocket. He took the cigarette with him. Finn cursed silently.

The doors clicked shut in succession, two layers protecting them from the racket inside.

"Why did you have to do that?"

"Do what?" She was curling the sides of his hair in her

fingers, even though it was too short.

"I was having a good conversation."

"As good as this?" She kissed his neck. A constellation winked in and out above him. He kept his eyes trained on it. Her pressure was muted, as if a feather was brushing up against him instead. His mouth tasted like coconut water, and if Sarah hadn't touched him with her frozen hands, he was sure his skin would've felt toasty with sun.

She started undoing his belt.

"Sarah. Somebody could come out."

"So? You love me, right?"

He blinked.

She sat back when he didn't answer. He couldn't afford Love. She knew that.

"That wasn't rhetorical, you know."

"Sarah..."

She waited, giving him a second chance. He didn't take it.

"I can't believe you," she said, wiping tears from her face. She pushed her body off his, not bothering to fix his belt. The doors slammed shut behind her once, then twice.

Finn felt fine where he was. The stairs were a hammock, and the dirt below him, soft sand. Why would he want Love ruining his life? He was fine with his run-of-the-mill emotions. The last time he took Happiness, his left eye hadn't stopped twitching for a week.

A star blinked in and out. He watched, waiting for it to happen again.

* * *

Finn was on his way to Mammy's the next day when he saw Elephant arguing with someone. A small girl was pouting, arms crossed tight, as Elephant gestured to the street.

"First time?" he asked the girl as he approached. Her clothes were grungy, and her synthetic black hair unkempt, but still, something bothered him. She was short and dirtied with makeup, but she had the unblemished complexion of a New Design. Her green eyes were big, accentuated by her thick lower lashes. Her lips were plush and the most perfect coral color. Her cheeks were round and smooth, and the space between her eyebrows, hairless. Underneath that baggy shirt...

She said nothing.

"Mammy's is referral only," Elephant grunted, crossing his arms back.

"That's why she was waiting for me. I'm her referral." Finn smiled, all teeth. "You know, Harry's is doing a two-for-one on mid-tier emotions right now."

Elephant scrutinized Finn before he waved down the barrier. "You're lucky I like you."

"You didn't have to do that," the girl said as they climbed the stairs.

"I don't mind."

He knew how desperate someone needed to be to end up at Mammy's, the cheapest shop in town. He also knew how much she must've spent to get her new skin and new features. He wanted to press her, but he also didn't want to scare her off.

"I'm Finn, by the way."

She hesitated before she replied. "Elsbeth."

"Need a tour?" he said as he held the door open for her. She gravitated toward the multicolored wall, laden with breakable emotions. Finn moved to her side. They stared at the array of colors.

"I'm going to try them all at some point."

"Yeah?" She was incredulous.

"You know what they say." He spread his arms out at the display. "Try everything once."

She looked at the wall. "Even... belittlement?"

"That one, I'd only try if the big kids were doing it too."

Her lips perked into a smile. Finn left her as he picked up his usual stash: a dropper of Charm, five tabs of Distraction, and a baggie full of powdered Adequacy. At the checkout counter, he took a handful of lollipops for good measure.

On their way out, Elsbeth pulled a vial from her bag.

"What's that?"

"No cheating," she said, wrapping it in his palm. The sloshing liquid was indistinguishable between yellow and orange. "Everything once, right?"

She left him next to Elephant. He opened his palm.

Curiosity.

"Oh, you're in trouble, aren't you?" Elephant asked.

* * *

Finn paid a pound for a vial of Love off a woman on Seventh Street. He knew it would taste terrible, and the color looked more beige than pink, but he wanted to try it. He couldn't afford the real stuff—never could and never would—but he'd grown used to Mammy's watered-down products, so what difference was something off the street?

He tossed it down his throat and continued his evening stroll through the metallic city. It was bitter at first, almost like Anger, but it had a sweet aftertaste. He hoped it wasn't laced with anything. He'd heard of Love-Exhilaration trips gone wrong, and that wasn't to mention the Happiness-Fear combo that killed a couple kids a year ago.

His sensations were heightened. He rubbed his pointer finger and his thumb together to test it. You could learn a lot about how an emotion was affecting you by how things felt. He could detect his own fingerprints, sense the dirt underneath his nails. The dose lasted him fifteen minutes, and it was mostly warmth and heart palpitations. He liked the Calm droplets better. Love's jittery feeling unnerved him.

He didn't think about Sarah once. Instead, he pictured Elsbeth, those big doe eyes and the black seeping from her hair. He wondered what Elsbeth had been like before the Re-Design. He wondered what she would feel like between his pointer finger and his thumb. Wondered what she'd feel like on Love. When he got home, he had a nibble of Boredom to level himself out.

The problem, though, was that everything tasted like chalk after Love, even the cheap stuff.

* * *

The next time he went to Mammy's, Elsbeth was smoking on the corner of the block. It was one of those new devices that made you feel like you were somewhere else, something about how it interacted with neurotransmitters and microchips. He had canceled his subscription to most of the chip's features months ago, but devices like that cost so much upfront, they worked for free.

"Want to try it?" she asked.

Today she was wearing ripped black tights and a T-shirt so big, it was a dress. Her boots were fancy leather, but the shoelaces were fraying. Her black hair had been tied back messily. He took a hit.

When he closed his eyes, he was in a dark, misty forest. Pine needles and dead leaves crunched underfoot. It smelled of evergreen. He couldn't see more than a couple meters in front of him as a dense fog approached. When he opened his eyes, the smell was the only thing that lingered.

"You're new around here, aren't you?" he asked.

"What gave it away?"

Her perfectly sculpted brow. Her faded freckles. Her expensive shoes. Her voice, the manufactured cadence somehow both soft and gritty. She sighed. "I was having some trouble at home. Needed a break, you know? How about you? You seem to know the place well. What brought you to Mammy's?"

He leaned against the wall, scratchy brick on his back, and laughed. "No one else would sell to me."

Her eyebrows perked up. "You're an Apath?"

"I don't like that word."

Many people had tried to use that term with him over the years. The doctors. (He didn't go back). His mates. (They were teasing, so it didn't really count). His parents. (They were just tired of him spending their money). Sarah. (As she moaned his name while they were high on Greed). Shop owners. (Selling to an Apath was license for closure).

"So, you can't feel anything without them?" Elsbeth asked.

"I wouldn't say that. I feel the wind on my cheek. I feel the wall biting into my back. I feel your arm close to mine."

She adjusted so there was more space between them. "And now?"

"I feel like you want to be an Apath. But New Designs don't need to, do they? They have everything built in."

She recoiled. "That's not true. We pay just like the rest of you."

Finn laughed. "At discounted prices."

"It's microdosing," she argued. "Nobody gets addicted."

"Is that why you left?" She snapped off the wall, but he continued. "It wasn't enough anymore. Nobody uptown would sell to the New Design girl. Nobody downtown wants to be caught dead with one, lest the department shuts them down. But you found out Mammy's doesn't care."

Her nostrils flared. He took her device once more, inhaling the foggy pinewood forest. It was dark and mystical. It filled his lungs with cedar. She could've chosen anywhere, anywhere in the world, but she picked there. He didn't have to ask why.

She liked the darkness. They had that in common.

As he exhaled, he handed it back to her with a folded-up note from his pocket.

"If you want to feel—really feel—you know where to find me."

* * *

Someone had scored Delight, and it was going around like a disease.

"Now this is the good stuff, eh?" Freud said as Finn came up from the kitchen table, wiping his nose. "Thank God for Xi and his rich mates."

Finn grinned. They were all secondary schoolmates, still living in the same neighborhood they used to tussle in. He was grateful for it. Who else would he get his real emotions from? They were on their way to becoming Apaths themselves, so they couldn't say anything.

Finn reached into his pocket, grabbing a fistful of lollipops, and then slammed them down onto the dusty table.

"What the fuck is this?" Freud asked when he saw the pile.

"Have you ever heard of roulette?" Finn was arranging them in a straight line, turning them over so their labels weren't visible. "Bottom of the millennium tradition. They did it with all sorts of things, I think."

The screen door creaked open and in came Sarah. Her eyeliner was smeared, and the tiny ensemble she wore, disheveled. They hadn't talked since the porch last time. Besides, she was dragging some new bloke in by the hand. She gave Finn a nasty side-eye.

The Delight was making him delirious as he shuffled the lollipops around, laughing.

"Go ahead," he told Freud. The man frowned but reached for the fifth down the line. He turned it over. It was Annoyance.

Finn cackled.

"You and your bloody lollis," Freud muttered as he unwrapped the bright red sphere, placing it in his mouth. His face contorted. "It's too salty. Your turn."

Finn swiveled his choice around so Freud could see. It was Confidence.

"Oh, fuck you," the man said.

Finn popped it into his mouth. It burned, but the pain faded after a couple seconds. It was tangerine colored and tasted like fruit too. As much as he hated True Designs and everything they stood for, they had mastered their recipes.

"Finn," Xi said from behind him. "Someone's looking for you."

Elsbeth stood by Xi's side. She had put something

shimmery on her eyelids, and her hair fell onto her face in coquettish layers. Her black lace dress hugged her constructed frame just right. She was angelic, all dark lines and creamy flesh. Standing next to the No Designs (a name Finn and his friends had made up for themselves), she was an airbrushed painting.

Sarah caught notice, her glare sharpening.

"You came," he said when Xi had stepped away. Elsbeth took the lollipop from his mouth and placed it in her own. Her voice held an alluring cadence as she said, "Don't make me regret it."

Everything was beautiful at Freud's. The music was loud and pumping. He took Elsbeth's hand in his, and they danced together. Her skin felt like skin. Her breath, like breath. When he examined her side profile, he noticed dead skin peppering the arches of her eyebrows. Her green eyes were marred by flakes of yellow.

But everything was beautiful. She was beautiful, pressed into him.

"So, Elsbeth," he asked. "What made you become a New Design?"

She pursed her lips together. If she wanted to play it off, she was in the wrong part of town.

"I didn't really have a choice," she conceded. "My parents work in the Influence sector. There's not much to want for when you have everything."

Maybe the statement would've revolted him if the Delight hadn't hit.

"So, *Finn*," she enunciated. "What made you become an Apath?"

He stole the lollipop back from her.

"A shitty childhood," he lied. It was boredom, more than anything. A deadbeat job in data collection and a string of disinteresting romantic entanglements. His parents thought kicking him out of the house would help, but it just made him lazier as he rented out his brother's place, who let him be late on his payments. Relics of the past were the only things Finn was truly interested in.

He hesitated. "Maybe I didn't have a choice, either."

When the lollipop had dissolved, he took her out to the porch, making sure both doors were shut tightly behind them, and then gave her his last line of Elation. How many emotions had he mixed at this point? It didn't matter. He craved the unpredictable outcome at the end of each night.

When he put her onto his lap, her pupils were huge, and her hair caught in his mouth. His vision was bright and distorted, filled with the twinkle of the inconsistent stars and the flash of Elsbeth's pale neck. He was bursting with fire from the stimulants, a combination of bad interplay in his liver and utter gratification.

"Feel it yet?" he asked as she rocked her hips.

"Yeah," she said.

"Yeah?"

"Yeah."

* * *

When he got home that night, he went straight to his nightstand. The blue-gray vial he bought at Mammy's was waiting for him there. He had shoved it far back, to keep it safe and hidden. He had wanted it out of sight, somewhere it could be forgotten. But he hadn't forgotten about it.

When he retrieved it, he tilted it over to see the label on

the bottom. It had a New Design label. This was the pure kind; he could tell by how the seal around the cap hadn't been broken yet.

It was Anguish. Nobody wanted it at the posh shops. The shitty ones, either. He sipped it, slow at first. It bubbled and fizzed going down, ice cold. When he couldn't stand it anymore, he tipped the rest down his gullet, letting his insides freeze.

Maybe he didn't need Love. Maybe this was enough.

* * *

Discussion Questions

1. If you had to take the pure form of an emotion, what three would you take and why? What is one you would never take and why?
2. What do you think is the purpose of emotions? How do you think society would be different if we didn't feel emotions? Would society be better, worse, or just different?
3. How are the emotion drugs in the story different than the ways people feed themselves emotions in real life? What's the difference (*if anything*) between taking a hit of "joy" and modern "retail therapy," gambling, dancing, or video games? Should they be judged differently or the same?
4. If the drugs in the story were real, would you ever do them? Why or why not? What other people in society do you think would do them and why?
5. If a person was a natural Apath and incapable of feeling emotions, do you think they should take the emotion drugs so they could attempt to live a more normal life?

* * *

S p e c t e r

Alexis Ames

* * *

<u>**Content Disclosure**</u>: Sexual Innuendo; Death or Bereavement; Suicidal Themes; Strong Language

* * *

It had been such a goddamn *stupid* way to die.

Noemi Markova, world-renowned mountaineer, who counted among her accomplishments scaling the tallest peak on every continent before the age of twenty, had been bested by a flight of *stairs*. There one moment, gone the next.

* * *

It wasn't difficult to obtain Noemi's body. Yasmeen signed paperwork until her hand cramped, but after that, the body was released into her custody so she could carry out the funerary practices Noemi had stipulated in her will. The body was to lie on a pad in their living room, blankets tucked around it as though Noemi were asleep, and their friends and family would fill the house. They would all grieve together with Noemi's body in the room with them. They would tell stories, sing songs, hug the body, stroke Noemi's hair. She would have a green burial after that, and her composted remains would feed their garden.

Yasmeen and Noemi's friends and family swiftly converged on their mountain town. A handful of sports outlets phoned the house to discuss her passing, calls that were fielded by someone else so Yasmeen could be with Noemi. *Outside Magazine* sent someone to take photographs and conduct a few interviews; that same night, a profile of world-renowned mountaineer Noemi Markova appeared on their website. It was everything Noemi would have wanted for her death, except for the way in which she had died.

Two days later, after the final mourner had left, Yasmeen loaded Noemi's body into the bed of her truck and brought her to the lab.

Élan vital, Yasmeen had been calling it. Vital force. A serum that so far had reanimated dead cells, insects, plants, and a rat. It was far from ready, human trials hadn't even been authorized yet, but there was no time. Ninety-six hours was the cutoff mark, and Noemi had been dead for ninety-two.

She hadn't expected her first test subject to be her wife.

* * *

"What did you do?"

Noemi sat on the edge of the table, her hands around her neck, the neck that had been broken in three places before the serum had snapped the vertebrae back into place and knit them together.

"You fell down the *stairs*, Noemi." Yasmeen sat slumped in a chair, elbows on her knees, her head in her hands. Exhaustion was a physical weight, like her bones had been infused with lead. When was the last time she'd slept? "I did what I had to."

"I—" Noemi pulled her hands away from her neck and stared at them. "I was going downstairs to get the laundry. I don't remember anything after that."

"You slipped. You fell. I found you when I got home. It was so fucking *stupid*."

The inside of Noemi's elbow was purpling, a ring with the injection site at the center. Noemi touched the bruise lightly, then pressed her thumb hard against it. A wince flickered across her face.

"I'm alive," she whispered.

Yasmeen gripped her hands tightly, relishing the way Noemi's fingers turned white as she squeezed the blood from them. The blood that was now coursing through her veins thanks to the heart that was beating in her chest.

"You're alive," Yasmeen said fiercely, "and I'm going to keep it that way."

* * *

Yasmeen drove Noemi from the lab back to their house in the dead of night. She then half-carried her inside and up to their bedroom. Exhaustion had hit Noemi like a ton of bricks, and Yasmeen suspected it was a side effect of the serum. She slept hard that night and through the next morning, only resurfacing in the midafternoon.

The dog sniffed Noemi curiously when she came downstairs, and immediately his ears went flat, his tail tucking itself between his legs. He darted off, and they found him under the dining room table. Noemi spent the better part of an hour trying to coax him out with treats and baby talk, but he refused to budge. He came out only when she finally left to shower and allowed Yasmeen to pet his trembling form.

"What's gotten into you?" she murmured. "That's *Noemi*."

Aside from that hiccup, the first few days after Noemi's revival were almost normal. Yasmeen did the shopping, and Noemi did the cooking. Noemi worked out in the makeshift gym in their basement or curled up in her chair near the fireplace with a book. Yasmeen worked on some reports in her home office and took the dog out for walks.

In the evenings, Noemi sat on the couch with her knitting while they watched television, her feet tucked under Yasmeen's thigh, glasses perched low on her nose. It had been a hobby of hers long before they met, but there was something off about her knitting now—she would fumble, sometimes even dropping the needles, and her creations started to take on a misshapen quality.

"My hands don't feel right," she admitted to Yasmeen, flexing her fingers. When Yasmeen took them, they were cold to the touch. "They're numb, and I can't move them like I used to."

Despite running every blood test she could think of, Yasmeen couldn't find an explanation for it.

She returned to work after her bereavement leave was up. Her colleagues gave her a wide berth, expressing their mumbled condolences but otherwise largely leaving her alone. She changed her schedule so she was in the lab three days a week and spent two at home, to maximize the time she got to spend with Noemi. After nearly losing *everything*, she wasn't about to squander a single moment with her wife.

The dog never approached Noemi willingly after that

first day at home. Whenever she entered a room, he fled, preferring the safety of his crate to sharing space with Noemi.

* * *

One fall afternoon, a neighbor called to let Yasmeen know that a fence in the back of their property had been damaged by a fallen branch. Yasmeen thanked her and went to pull on her boots and coat. Noemi followed her.

"What are you doing?"

"I'm going with you."

"You aren't," Yasmeen said. "You can't leave the house."

"There's no one around!"

"The neighbors are," Yasmeen pointed out. "They saw that our fence is broken; you think they won't notice when I go out there with you at my side? Your hair alone is recognizable from a mile away."

"I'll wear a hat."

"Noemi, you cannot be seen under any circumstances! Christ, can you imagine the kind of riot *that* would start? World-renowned mountaineer Noemi Markova, who had broken her neck falling down the stairs not three days ago, being spotted out and about in *Aspen*? The *chaos* that would ensue would be extraordinary, not to mention that I'd lose my job, my lab, be stripped of *everything*—"

"Why did you bring me back, Yasmeen?" Noemi asked, throwing her arms up. "I can't leave the house, I can't be seen in public or by any of our friends and family, I can't do what I was put on this Earth to do. What kind of an existence is that?"

"You have *me*," Yasmeen said heatedly. "You have me, you have this beautiful home, our dog, the life we built together—"

"Yes, I have this beautiful home, the dog who can't stand

to be near me, and a wife who won't let me leave the house," Noemi said. "What kind of life is it if I'm trapped in here for the rest of it? What do you expect me to do, knit my days away? Why did you bring me *back*?"

"I brought you back because I love you!" Yasmeen burst out. "Because I refuse, *refuse* to be a widow at forty-nine. Because you've scaled the most dangerous mountains in the world and died falling down the *stairs*. It was a senseless way to die, Noemi! It was a *waste*."

"So now you'll keep me in here, where I'll waste away to nothing instead. That's the better death for you?"

"I'm not talking about this," Yasmeen said, wrenching the door open.

* * *

Weeks passed.

Noemi didn't touch her knitting.

The dog refused to come near her.

* * *

One afternoon, Yasmeen returned from work to an eerily silent house. It was reminiscent of the chilled, foreboding silence that had greeted her the night she discovered Noemi's body, and her heart jammed in her throat.

She found Noemi in the bathtub, shivering with cold, the bloodred water up to her waist. A razor blade lay abandoned on the side of the tub, and Noemi was staring at her wrists.

"It didn't work," she whispered as Yasmeen plunged her hand into the water to pull the plug. "I... cut them, but they... it didn't work."

Yasmeen grabbed a towel and draped it over Noemi's shoulders before helping her out of the tub. Noemi was still shivering violently, and Yasmeen wrapped the towel fully around her before hugging her close.

"What were you *thinking*?" she whispered into Noemi's damp hair. The air was heavy and metallic, and it made her stomach churn.

"I-I can't die," Noemi stuttered, pressing her fingers to her unblemished wrists. "Oh, my God. I *can't die*."

* * *

Whenever Yasmeen spoke to their nieces and nephews, Noemi sat on the other side of the table, out of sight of the camera. Listening but never speaking up, lingering on the periphery of every conversation. She would put a hand over her mouth whenever she heard her sister's voice, as though she physically needed to hold the words at bay.

She stopped cooking meals, claiming it didn't matter what she made, all food tasted the same to her nowadays.

Throughout the day, she drifted from room to room. Yasmeen would often find her on the western side of the house, staring out at the unattainable mountains that once had been her second home. Sometimes it was like she wasn't there at all— Yasmeen would call her name, would ask her a question, and Noemi wouldn't react. She wouldn't even blink, and Yasmeen knew Noemi hadn't even heard her.

* * *

Noemi's touch was cold. Her fingertips were chilled against Yasmeen's bare skin, a series of icy pinpricks as she trailed her fingers over Yasmeen's chest and down her stomach. Even her tongue was cold where it pressed against Yasmeen, but the shock of it only heightened her arousal, made her come harder than she had in years.

She knew Noemi's body as well as her own, knew what turned her on and made her writhe, but Noemi hadn't had an orgasm since her resurrection. When mouth and tongue and fingers failed her, Yasmeen resorted to toys, but none of them worked. Noemi's body remained frustratingly unresponsive, and eventually, they stopped trying at all.

* * *

Streaks of gray soon began to highlight Yasmeen's once-dark hair, and wrinkles deepened in her cheeks and around her eyes and mouth. Age had crept up on her; she hadn't noticed it in the haze of the past several months, not until she caught sight of a photograph of herself in *Human Molecular Genetics* and thought for a moment that it was her mother.

She looked in the mirror and realized with a jolt that she looked older than Noemi.

"How is it that I have more gray hairs than you do?" she said over breakfast one morning, forcing a laugh that sounded lighter than she felt and running a hand through her hair. "I seem to have lost the genetic lottery."

Noemi just looked resigned. "It's not genetics."

"Darling, what else could it be?"

"You're smarter than that, Yasmeen. You're more *observant* than that. You know exactly what this is."

* * *

When winter returned to the mountains, it was brutal, keeping them housebound more often than not. Noemi was more absent than ever, spending most of her days gazing at the mountains she would have been climbing and skiing in another lifetime.

One morning, Yasmeen woke to find Noemi's side of the

bed empty and cold. She couldn't smell coffee or breakfast, but the sun was already over the trees, and a stone grew in her stomach.

She searched the entire house to no avail. No snow had fallen overnight, so when she flung open the back door, Noemi's boot prints through the snow were clearly visible. Yasmeen threw on her gear and trudged out into the bright white on snowshoes. It took her the better part of an hour to follow Noemi's footsteps up one of the foothills, where she found her wife half-frozen and huddled in the snow.

By the time Yasmeen got her back to the house, it was nearly noon. She wrapped Noemi in blankets and towels, and finally coaxed her upstairs into a warm bath. She wasn't concerned about Noemi losing her life again—by now, she knew it wouldn't happen. But Noemi *did* still experience pain and discomfort, and that was what Yasmeen hoped to ease.

Anger didn't come until much later when Noemi was dry and dressed and staring out the windows once more.

"How can you keep doing this to me?" Yasmeen demanded. "Don't you understand I did it for you? For us?"

"For *me*?" Noemi shot back incredulously. "You didn't bring me back for anyone other than *yourself.*"

"How can you say that?" Yasmeen asked. "Was that the ending you wanted? World-renowned climber Noemi Markova dies falling down the stairs—*that's* the bookend you wanted on your life?"

"What does it matter? I can never leave this house. I can never interact with anyone in the world again. As far as everyone is concerned, I *did* die falling down the stairs, and bringing me back won't fix that!"

"We were supposed to grow old together!"

"Thanks to you, I'm never going to grow old at *all*! Do you realize how cruel that is, bringing me back so I would watch *you* die instead?"

"I didn't." Yasmeen's face was hot, and her eyes burned. "I didn't *know*."

"And what the hell do you expect me to do once you're— once you're no longer here?" Noemi folded her arms. "I'm *dead*. I have no documentation, no identification, nothing. My degrees and resume are useless because they belong to a dead woman. You brought me back from the dead, but this is no life, Yasmeen."

The argument fizzled out as quickly as it had started. When Noemi left the room, it was silent, as though she hadn't been there at all.

Yasmeen was living with a ghost. A ghost who wouldn't die, *couldn't* die.

It wasn't the dead who haunted her after all. It was the living.

* * *

Discussion Questions

1. Noemi should be dead, doesn't age, can't leave the house, and can't die. How would you rank the level of wrongness for these or other issues related to Yasmeen bringing Noemi back from the dead?

2. Yasmeen argues she didn't know the full extent of the serum's side effects. Does that matter in deciding the ethics of bringing her partner back from the dead related to the various issues in question one? For example, would Yasmeen be less culpable if Noemi had come back completely normal and continued aging like a normal person?

3. Is bringing the dead back to life a medical technology line that should never be crossed? What (*if anything*) is the difference between reviving someone who had been dead seventeen hours (*the current confirmed record*) versus the ninety-two hours in the story?

4. Do the following factors affect your willingness to allow a dead person to be revived: the way a person dies, the age of the person, or the unfinished business in their life? If so, why?

5. What percentage of loving spouses, given the opportunity, would do the exact same thing Yasmeen did in the story? Does that percentage matter when creating potential prohibition laws?

* * *

One Out of Four

Joseph S. Klapach

* * *

Content Disclosure: Death or Bereavement; Moderate Intensity, Mild Language

* * *

Molly circled the date of her eighteenth birthday on her calendar. She was tired of being told she had a "pretty face." She was tired of being told she was "funny" and "kind" and "smart," and that those were the "most important things." Her class had even voted her "Best Personality," as a superlative, but she knew what that meant. She overheard Danny and Aiden talking after the assembly. "Molly's got a great personality," Danny said loud enough for everyone to hear. "A great, big personality. A larger-than-life personality." And Aiden burst out laughing as Danny stuck out his arms and waddled down the hallway like a penguin.

Molly made the appointment in secret on her seventeenth birthday. Of course, her parents had forbidden her from going anywhere near the clinic. "We know you'll be tempted," they told her. "But it would break our hearts if anything happened to you." "It isn't worth the risk," her father warned. "One-quarter of all patients," her mother added. "That's one out of four." "Look at us," her father boasted. "We're happy, and we've never had the shot."

But Molly didn't care. She couldn't wait to take Diovix.

On the morning of her eighteenth birthday, Molly snuck out of the house and caught a rideshare to the downtown clinic. She left her parents a note saying she was studying at the library, so they wouldn't worry or try to stop her. She skipped breakfast like the clinic recommended, and her stomach was growling audibly by the time she crossed the Liberty Bridge.

When Molly arrived at the clinic, she was surprised to see so many protesters. She had hoped to avoid any unwanted attention by scheduling an early appointment, but the protesters were a dedicated bunch. Even at eight a.m., over a hundred people crowded behind the ropes that lined the sidewalk in front of the clinic. Some of the protesters sang. Others waved placards with messages like "Don't do it!" and "God loves you the way you are." It felt like every single one of them was staring at Molly as she braved the gauntlet between the street and the clinic.

"Hey, I like your sweater," one of the protesters shouted. It was a girl about Molly's age. Maybe a year or two older. The girl spoke with an air of presumed familiarity. Like they had been assigned as roommates at summer camp.

"I'm Lisa," the girl continued. "I can't imagine what you're feeling, but I want you to know there are lots of us who support you." The girl walked alongside Molly, just behind the ropes. "We think real beauty isn't something you can see from the outside, and real happiness doesn't come from how you look."

Molly had read an article about how to deal with protesters. She said nothing and kept her eyes trained on the clinic.

"If you're having any second thoughts, I'm happy to talk. We could grab coffee. There's a great place around the corner."

Molly ignored the girl and focused on the clinic.

"It's a big decision. Think it through before you do anything you might regret."

The girl reached the end of the roped-off area, but that didn't stop her from calling out after Molly.

"Look me up when you realize drugs can't cure loneliness. I'm @lovingwhoiam."

And, finally, Molly was inside the clinic.

Molly's first thought when she came through the revolving doors was that it felt more like she was visiting a day spa at a fancy hotel than a medical facility. The clinic's atrium boasted high, vaulted ceilings topped with a glass dome that bathed the foyer's warm, earthen tones in natural light. The furniture was sleek, modern, and inviting. The couch's sensuous curves seemed to beckon for Molly to sit down, relax, and flip through a magazine.

Molly checked in for her appointment, and the receptionist advised her that a service coordinator would be with her momentarily. As Molly waited, she tapped her feet nervously on the reception room's elegant marble tile. The scent of lavender and lilac filled the air, and the sound of running water gurgled from a fountain built into an alcove. Molly glanced at a pamphlet on a nearby coffee table. On the pamphlet's cover, an attractive man and woman ran together through a field of wildflowers. Above the couple hung the words: "Welcome to the rest of your life."

After a few minutes, a tall, angular woman with a distinctly Scandinavian appearance emerged from a back room and approached Molly with a cordial smile.

"Good morning. Are you Molly Durham?" the woman asked. Molly answered in the affirmative. "I'm Janine, and I will be coordinating your visit. We are delighted to have you with us today."

The woman shook Molly's hand and then made a sweeping gesture toward a nearby staircase.

"Please accompany me upstairs to review the arrangements for your treatment."

Molly followed Janine up the stairs. As they ascended, Molly found that Janine's tiny waist was directly in her line of sight. Molly averted her eyes, only to find herself looking instead at Janine's shapely calves and expensive heels. To make matters worse, something about the staircase's angle of incline caused Molly to feel the full weight of her body, and she was forced to pause briefly at a bend to catch her breath. When they reached the second floor, Janine ushered Molly into a conference room. Janine sat down at the head of a stately boardroom table with a polished, granite top. Molly joined Janine, taking the seat to her left.

"You're scheduled this morning for your first Diovix treatment. As I'm sure you already know, Diovix is a revolutionary weight loss drug. Diovix will reset your body's metabolism and boost your biochemical functions to ensure that you maintain a perfectly calibrated, predetermined weight."

Janine produced a tablet and scrolled through the intake

form Molly had submitted online.

"Given your height and frame, your target weight will be 120 pounds. No matter how much you eat or drink, Diovix will adjust your basal metabolic rate to keep you at your target weight. As long as you take Diovix, you will never have to worry about unwanted weight gain. You will always be exactly 120 pounds."

Janine paused for a few seconds before continuing in a firmer tone.

"I've told you the good. Now it's time for the bad.

"First, seventy-five percent of the patients who use Diovix do not experience any side effects, but for the other twenty-five percent, the side effects are severe and irreversible. Death is immediate; it is painful; and it is unstoppable. For a quarter of the population, Diovix is simply incompatible with their body chemistry. We don't know why it happens, but it does. And, despite our best efforts, we have not yet been able to screen our patients in advance to determine which ones will suffer adverse reactions. If you go forward with your Diovix treatment today, there is a twenty-five percent chance you will die.

"Second, Diovix does not work overnight. Given your current weight, it will take at least six months for you to reach your target weight. During that time, you will lose around five pounds each week, as your body gradually acclimates to the treatment. You need to have realistic expectations. You will not wake up tomorrow weighing 120 pounds. I promise you will get there eventually, but you will have to be patient during your journey.

"Third, Diovix wears off. To maintain your target weight, you will need a booster shot every two years. We do offer prepayment packages. There's a five percent discount if you purchase ten years of booster shots and a ten percent discount if you purchase twenty years of booster shots, but there's no getting around the fact that Diovix is not simply a drug. It's a lifestyle.

"Fourth, we cannot make any guarantees about your figure. Some of our patients have grown accustomed to having larger breasts, ample curves, tapered waistlines, and heart-shaped bottoms. Diovix causes uniform weight loss across your entire body. It will keep you at 120 pounds, but that weight loss may come at the expense of your favorite features. For this reason, some of our patients choose to augment their Diovix treatments with plastic surgery. That, of course, is beyond the scope of the services we provide.

"Finally, the administration of the Diovix treatment is heavily regulated. There is a legally mandated one-hour 'cooling-off' period between when you sign your contract with us and the actual administration of the treatment. During this waiting period, you have the right to change your mind and withdraw from the treatment at any time, and you will receive a full refund for any amounts you have paid. No questions asked.

"We are also required by law to administer all our initial Diovix injections to patients in groups of four. This means that even if you do not personally experience any side effects from Diovix, you may witness someone else who does."

Janine lifted the tablet and pointed it at Molly's face. Molly could see the green light blinking on the tablet's camera.

"Molly Durham, having been fully informed about Diovix, including the substantial risk of death, do you wish to proceed with the treatment?"

"Yes, I do," Molly answered.

"Have you been advised of your legal right to withdraw from the treatment with a full refund at any time during the one-hour waiting period?"

"I have," Molly said.

"Have you been advised that you will receive the Diovix treatment with other patients and that you may witness someone else experiencing the side effects of Diovix?"

"I have," Molly repeated.

"Terrific," Janine said. "Let's take care of the paperwork, but first I'll need to see your ID."

Molly handed Janine her license, which Janine ran through a holo-scanner.

"It's just a formality," Janine said while the scanner whirred. "You wouldn't believe how many minors we get with fake IDs."

The holo-scanner chirped positively.

"Oh, happy birthday!" Janine gushed as she gave Molly back her license. "I got my first Diovix injection on my eighteenth birthday too."

Janine caught herself and returned to a demeanor of efficient professionalism.

"Next, we have the consent forms."

Janine placed the tablet in front of Molly, handed her a stylus, and guided her through a seemingly endless number of forms. Some of the forms disclosed the risks of treatment. Others released the clinic from liability. There was even something about arbitration.

"We're almost done," Janine said at last. "All that's left is payment for the procedure."

Molly reached into her purse and took out a thick envelope. She could see a flicker of annoyance in Janine's eyes, but Janine dutifully counted each well-worn bill. The envelope represented ten years of birthdays and Christmases, eight years of babysitting, and four years of double shifts at Subway.

When Janine finished counting, she led Molly to a changing room. Molly stuffed her belongings into a locker and put on a white terry cloth bathrobe. Afterward, Janine escorted Molly to a private examination room. The room had sage-green walls, charcoal cabinets, and what looked like an adjustable massage chair. Janine wished Molly well and said goodbye.

Almost as soon as Janine left, a nurse bustled into the room. The nurse asked Molly to remove her robe, sit down in the chair, and hold as still as possible. While Molly sat, the nurse activated a holo-scanner built into the chair. The scanner tickled Molly's skin as it ran slowly along the contours of her body. Periodically, the nurse's tablet chimed. Molly caught a glimpse of the tablet's screen when the nurse bent over to adjust the position of one of Molly's legs. The screen displayed Molly's height and weight, her blood pressure, the oxygen levels in her blood, and various figures relating to her bone structure, density, and mass. After the holo-scan, the nurse produced a small device and asked Molly to extend her right hand.

"This is called a lancet," the nurse explained. "It has a tiny needle that is going to prick your finger and extract a tiny bit of blood that the lab will use to formulate your Diovix shot. You'll just feel a little pinch."

The nurse took the blood sample, wrapped Molly's finger in a small bandage, and waited patiently while Molly got out of the chair and put her robe back on.

"Now we're off to the treatment room," the nurse said cheerfully.

The treatment room was the first place that felt like a doctor's office. It was a rectangular suite with four stainless steel reclining chairs. Flat-screen monitors were affixed to the wall directly in front of each chair.

Two patients were already there when Molly arrived. A portly Italian man in his forties sat in the first chair with his eyes scrunched shut. The man clung tightly to the armrests on his chair and muttered feverishly to himself. As Molly drew closer, she could make out the words.

"Holy Mary, Mother of God, pray for us sinners, now and at the hour of our death."

A heavyset young man sat in the second chair. He had chubby cheeks and an unfortunate buzz cut that made his head appear square shaped. Although he was seated, Molly could tell he was an enormous mountain of a man. He had broad shoulders, thick arms, tree trunks for legs, and a body shaped like a giant barrel. Given his size, his boyish features, and his terrible haircut, he reminded Molly of a baby-faced Frankenstein.

The nurse directed Molly to sit in the third chair.

"Thank God," the baby-faced Frankenstein said to Molly. "I was afraid I'd be stuck all by myself with the pope here."

Frankenstein jerked his head in the direction of the praying Italian.

"I'm Michael," the young man said. "Michael Schroeder. But everyone calls me Schroeds."

"I'm Molly," she replied.

"Oh, like the Unsinkable Molly Brown." Schroeds tapped rhythmically on the chair's armrest with his large, stubby fingers. "She was the OG badass, boss girl. Look her up."

Schroeds extended his arm toward Molly and offered her a fist bump.

"Nice to meet you, Molly," Schroeds said. "You go to Pitt?"

"In the fall." Molly bumped his fist. "I'm about to graduate high school."

"Allegheny High? Or Baldwin?"

"Neither. I'm just outside the city."

"Where?"

"Moon Township."

"I love it," Schroeds said, still tapping his stubby fingers. "I'm going to call you Molly the Moon Girl."

Molly laughed. She was grateful for the distraction.

The door opened, and a nurse entered with another patient. This one was a skinny redheaded woman in her early thirties. She wore dark sunglasses and a ballcap and carried herself like a celebrity who was ashamed of being caught somewhere scandalous by the paparazzi. The woman gave Molly and Schroeds a look of thinly veiled disgust as she passed by.

"Hey, we're not crazy about being stuck with you either," Schroeds snapped at the redhead. "I mean, I've had shits bigger than you."

"That's enough," the nurse snarled.

"Certainly, my dear Nurse Ratched." Schroeds made a loud farting noise and shot Molly a conspiratorial wink.

"I hope I don't get sent down to the principal's office," he whispered.

After the redhead had taken her seat, the nurse spoke to the four patients.

"You are all here for your first Diovix treatment. State law requires that we play a video for you during the waiting period that discusses the potential side effects of Diovix. You have the right, but not the obligation, to watch this video."

The nurse walked down the line of chairs and handed earbuds to each of the patients.

"Psh," Schroeds hissed, tossing the earbuds onto a metal tray affixed to his chair. "I already saw everything I needed to make my decision when I looked in the mirror this morning."

Molly glanced up at the screen in front of her. A man in a white lab coat sat behind a wooden desk and spoke to the camera with the utmost seriousness. After a moment's hesitation, Molly set her earbuds down on her chair's metal tray.

"You ever watch Hella Dumb?" Schroeds asked Molly.

"Never heard of it."

"Posted a great one last week. It's my favorite streamer." Schroeds reached into his bathrobe's pocket and produced a cell phone. "Just look at this." He clicked an app, flipped his phone to the side, and held it out for Molly to see. "It's a zoo in China," Schroeds narrated. "All their pandas died, so they painted these Chow Chows white and black and tried to pass them off as pandas."

Molly laughed. Those dogs weren't going to fool anyone.

"I got a brilliant idea when I saw this," Schroeds bragged. "You have any little brothers or sisters?"

"Only child, but I babysit for the neighbors."

"Perfect," Schroeds said. "I want you to picture it in your head. Close your eyes. Take a deep breath. Now imagine you're taking the neighbors' kids to the zoo. What are their names, by the way?"

"Liam and Emily."

"So you're taking Liam and Emily to the zoo, but instead of lions and tigers and elephants, the entire zoo is full of puppies painted to look like other animals. There's a golden retriever dyed with stripes to look like a tiger, a mastiff shaved to look like a lion, a greyhound speckled to look like a leopard, and a chihuahua with little white spots like a fawn. And the poodle puppies are the best. They've been trimmed and colored to look like zebras, camels, and even giraffes."

Schroeds clasped Molly's arm with his gigantic palm. Molly opened her eyes and looked at him.

"But instead of just watching the animals, like at a regular zoo, the kids at my zoo can play with my puppies for as long as they want."

Schroeds's baby face was full of earnest excitement.

"And when I make my first billion dollars off my puppy zoo franchise, I'll whisk you away to the Oscars in a flying car."

"Why would the Puppy Zoo King take me to the Oscars?" Molly asked.

"Because you're gonna star in all the movies I produce, duh."

Before Molly could respond, Schroeds was flipping through more reels.

"Have you ever seen 'Interviews with Garden Gnomes'? Or, how about Gunther Walz's mini-histories? My favorites are his 'Condensed Chronicle of Condensed Milk' and his 'Abridged Account of the Dixon Bridge Disaster.'"

"What part of the internet do you lurk?"

"The best part," Schroeds bragged.

Schroeds showed Molly a series of reels. Of course, he narrated each one enthusiastically. They were in the middle of watching a crudely drawn, animated horse explain why there aren't any unicorns when a doctor and four nurses entered the waiting room. Schroeds flipped his phone off and stowed it back in the pocket of his robe.

The doctor walked down the line of chairs asking each patient the same question: "You have now completed the one-hour waiting period. Do you still wish to proceed with the Diovix treatment?"

"Yes," mumbled the Italian.

"Hell, yeah," shouted Schroeds.

"Yes, sir," answered Molly.

"Uh-huh," nodded the redhead.

The doctor returned to the first chair. One of the nurses presented a tray with four syringes. Another nurse rolled up the sleeve of the Italian's bathrobe. The Italian made the sign of the cross with his free hand and began praying even more fervently.

"Hail Mary, full of grace, the Lord is with thee. Blessed art thou amongst women and blessed is the fruit of thy womb, Jesus."

The doctor injected the syringe into the exposed underside of the Italian's arm. The Italian stopped praying and sat absolutely still. Then, he opened his eyes slowly and exhaled loudly.

"Congratulations, Mr. Rossi," the doctor said. "Betsy will show you to the recovery room."

A nurse helped the Italian to his feet, and they exited the waiting room together.

The doctor moved on to the second chair.

"Give me a hit of that Fountain of Youth," Schroeds said. The doctor raised a syringe and studied it briefly while a nurse rolled up Schroeds's sleeve. Schroeds smiled at Molly.

"Geronimo!" he exclaimed.

The doctor injected the syringe into the underside of Schroeds's arm. Schroeds sat motionless for a moment. Then, he looked down at his hand.

"Why can't I—" Schroeds said. His arm was trembling.

"I'm sorry, son." The doctor gripped Schroeds tightly on the shoulder.

That's when all chaos broke loose. Schroeds vomited all over the front of his terry cloth robe and started convulsing uncontrollably. Every part of his body quivered, and his spine arched so forcefully that only the back of his Frankenstein head remained touching his chair.

"Oh, my God!" the redhead shrieked. She leaped to her feet so fast the sunglasses flew off her face.

Schroeds continued shaking violently. The doctor and nurses tried to hold him down, but he was too big and too powerful for them to control. His giant body shuddered, and he tossed one of the nurses aside like a bull tossing a rider at a rodeo.

"Let me out!" the redhead screamed.

Schroeds's whole body rocked and rattled and twisted like a ship on rough seas. Somehow, he managed to turn himself onto his side, facing Molly.

"Let me out!" the redhead repeated before collapsing in hysterics onto the floor.

"Get her out of here," the doctor barked at one of the

nurses.

Schroeds let out a piteous, guttural howl.

"I don't want to," the redhead sobbed as a nurse hoisted her to her feet. "You can't make me."

Schroeds was staring directly at Molly. He tried to reach his hand out toward her, but it flopped aimlessly in awkward spasms.

The redhead emitted an ear-shattering screech.

"I said get her out of here!" the doctor yelled.

"Just my luck," Schroeds groaned.

The nurse shoved the redhead out the door.

And then Schroeds gazed at Molly with empty eyes.

The doctor grimaced, as if he had felt a sudden stab of pain. Then, he pushed a button on the wall. Almost immediately, the door popped open, and two attendants came in pushing a gurney. The attendants, the doctor, and the nurses lifted Schroeds's body out of the chair and laid him gently on the gurney. Molly could tell from the color of his robe that Schroeds had pissed himself.

"Notify the next of kin," the doctor instructed one of the nurses. The attendants wheeled Schroeds's body out. A nurse followed them.

"Do you wish to proceed with the treatment?" The doctor's voice was calm and professional, and it took Molly a moment to realize he was speaking to her.

"It's okay if you need to reschedule."

"No," Molly said in a quiet voice. "Give it to me. Please. I just want it to be over. One way or the other."

The last remaining nurse produced a syringe and handed it to the doctor.

"Are you sure?" the doctor asked.

"Yes," Molly replied.

The nurse rolled up Molly's sleeve, and the doctor gave Molly the injection. Molly sat quietly and then sighed in relief.

Molly could only remember snippets of what happened next. The doctor congratulated her. The nurse guided her into the recovery ward. Janine reappeared and handed her a sheet full of instructions. Then, suddenly, Molly was outside, in front of the clinic, stumbling toward a waiting rideshare.

"Hey, sweater girl," shouted a familiar voice. "I'm glad you made it, but you'll see. Diovix can't cure loneliness. Look me up when the fantasy wears off. It's @lovingwhoiam."

The next thing Molly knew, she was crossing the Liberty Bridge in the back seat of a rideshare. Molly felt both amped up and thoroughly exhausted. She leaned her head against the window and gazed out across the Monongahela River. There, at the edge of the horizon, just beyond the range of waking sight, she could almost see a glimmer of happiness.

* * *

Discussion Questions

1. Gastric Band Surgery, Ozempic, and their competitors all carry side effect risks, including death. How are the risks of current treatments the same, or different, than the side effect of death in the story? Are we just haggling over acceptable amounts of death in exchange for treatment?

2. Do you think the government regulations in the story—a one-hour waiting period and being forced to be in a room with others who get the treatment—are appropriate? What (*if any*) government regulations would you put into place?

3. It can certainly be argued that medical weight loss, while it carries risk, carries less risk than being severely overweight. However, what if the person is not overweight but simply wants to preemptively take Diovix to ensure they will never be overweight?

4. Do you think the protestors are right (*or should be allowed*) to be in front of the clinic attempting to guilt patients into changing their mind?

5. Can a person who has never been severely overweight fairly judge (*or regulate*) those who take Diovix? Is this equally true for other forms of medical or quality-of-life treatments?

* * *

Face Chopping

J.S. McQueen

* * *

<u>Content Disclosure</u>: Strong Language; Sexual Situations

* * *

When she opened the bookstore door the cold wind sliced through the warmth of the cafe. I was sitting by the electric fireplace, reading my copy of Moby Dick. I turned to see who walked inside because my paranoid ass always has to. The feminist in me is ashamed to say my eyes lay on her thighs first. She was wearing a short skirt and no leggings in the middle of a Chicago winter. Like it was *the snow* that needed to bundle up when *she* blew into town.

I quickly dragged my eyes up to her face. She was looking around the store with her sunglasses on, putting her fingers on the stick of the sucker in her mouth and pulling it out. Her beauty struck me like a bell. When her sunglasses found my eyes, I turned away and tried my best to look at my book and contain the feeling that was rapidly climbing up through my guts and into my throat.

"I wish I could look like that," I whispered.

I returned to reading the chapter of the book with all the sperm in it, when a flash of pink and white caught the top of my eyes, and I looked up to see her.

She popped the sucker out of her mouth. "Whatcha readin'?"

I could have choked on the saccharine of her voice. "What? Nothing."

She popped her lips and stared at me for a moment, and then pointedly turned her face toward the book I was holding. I caught the barest glimpse of her eyes in the shadow of her sunglasses, a strange blue hidden beneath luscious eyelashes before she turned back up to me.

"Oh. M-Moby Dick."

"Oo. Moby *Dick*," she said, rolling the words around in her mouth like a marble. "I always thought the name of that book was funny."

"Actually, it was on purpose, the author wanted people to, y'know, laugh. At. The uh. At the dick. Thing. The penis," I felt myself held hostage by the moment and by my own self, "it's. A gay book."

"Maybe it's a *tranny* book."

The word pinned me to my chair like an insect to a board. "What?" I said, my face flush with a mix of anger and humiliation.

"Y'know," she said, taking a lick from her lollipop, "because they spend the whole book trying to hunt down this dick. Maybe it's a metaphor for hating your own manhood. Ishmael is a pretty feminine guy, isn't he? Or, maybe I should say she." She giggled, and it was like raindrops on a frozen lake.

"Th-that's actually a pretty good interpreta—"

"Wanna go to a gay bar tonight?"

"H-huh?"

"Gay bar you, me, my friends, bar, gay."

"Did—were you gonna buy books or—"

"Just say yes," she said, dipping down into the low masculine registers of her vocal range. She's like me. She's trans too, except I couldn't tell. I couldn't tell at all. Not until she wanted me to.

I stared at her as my body crackled with a Molotov cocktail of indiscernible emotions. "Yes."

After we exchanged numbers and agreed to meet at a bar called Flush, I ran to the bathroom and locked myself in the handicapped stall so I had room to breathe. I was run over by a feelings stampede, and I was laughing and smiling while my body filled with so much rage. I pulled out my phone to use it as a mirror, looking at my own face. My bulging brow ridge, my massive nose, my square jaw. I knew then what it was. Loathing. I hated her.

How dare she get to look like that, walk in like she owned the ground she walked on, and just clock me in public. How dare she do that to me? My face was hot with tears, and a sob whined its way out of my throat. And then she tricked me into meeting her at a bar. I *hate* bars, but she pressured me, and so I agreed. I agreed because I'm an ugly doormat that looks like a man and hungers for even a scrap of attention from anyone.

I could text her. I could cancel. I pulled up her phone number and opened the text box and stared at it. Just cancel. You don't even fucking know her, just cancel. I opened up the keyboard and started typing. Christ, why did my fingers shake so much? I was only halfway through the message when I got a text from her.

"It was so awesome to meet another trans woman in the city. Sorry if I came off a little strong. Looking forward to hanging out with you tonight!!!"

My anger was squashed. My insides turned to soup. Waves of shame washed over me, put their hands on my shoulder, pushed my ass down to the tile of the bookstore bathroom floor, and tears trickled out of my throat. *She is weird, so am I,* I thought. *What am I doing? I'm better than this.*

I sat there for a long moment before getting to my feet. *It's just one night,* I thought. *I'll tell her later I don't like bars or meeting new people. That I went for her sake. Then we can be friends if she's okay with that.* My head ran away with me, pictures of us going to bookstores and talking about books, or her straddling me while I lay on the couch, crouched over me, doing my makeup the same way she did hers. *God her makeup was so good.*

My face turned red. Shit, my thoughts were getting away from me, don't get ahead of yourself you idiot, it's just a night in a bar. It's just. A night in a bar. It could lead to things, it could not, just remember what your therapist told you and take the present as it comes.

Take. The present. As it comes.

* * *

I was overwhelmed the second I walked into the bar by the sure knowledge that I had made a huge fucking mistake. It wasn't too crowded but I was immediately terrified the guy at the front door would see the M on my driver's license. Turned out the fear was unnecessary; I got sirred by the guy at the front before I even handed him my card. After that, I was terrified to walk through the crowd. I had even tried to put on makeup, which I hardly ever do because I suck at it, and the music and the voices and the lights were all so overwhelming I felt like a naked mole rat with a wig on. Even though it's my actual hair.

I was about to leave when I felt soft fingers and long nails curl around my arm. I turned to see her, still wearing those sunglasses.

She smiled a wide smile that showed off her glistening white canines. "You came."

"Yeah," I said, but she was already tugging at me, and I was following. She might as well have slapped a collar on me. I could have worn one of those muzzles for humans; at least that would have stopped me from putting my foot in my mouth.

"My friends," she said, gesturing at a table in a particularly dark corner.

"Oh my God," said a red-haired girl with a sparkling silver dress sitting on the edge of a booth. She put her drink down on the table.

Another, a purple-haired one in a crop top and low-rise jeans, laughed and said, "Look at her eyeliner. Girl, what did you *do*?"

I was instantly transported back to high school. It actually would have been easier if they just shoved me to the ground and called me a faggot.

"She's bricked as a shithouse," came another voice, a brunette in a dark red dress.

They all laughed at me, and I looked down at the woman who brought me here. I became shamefully and completely aware of how much taller I was than her. I had a half a foot on her at *least*. My humiliation gave birth to the return of a deep rage; she just brought me here to make fun of me.

Then I felt her fingers, cool as a breeze, wrap around my chin and pinch my cheeks together.

"Be nice you stupid whores," she said with a loud cackle.

They kept laughing but said, "Okay, okay."

She turned my face to hers, and I was helpless in her hands. My mind was burning with the desire to shove her away, to yell at her for putting her hands on me without asking, but I didn't. Instead, I was just turned on. So turned on.

"Your eyeliner is a mess. And you look like a man," she said, "but look girlies, there's potential here." She turned me to face them. "See?"

They leaned in closer to examine me. I felt like a freak in a cage.

"She does have good hair," said the redhead.

The brunette chimed in, "And your face has good symmetry. If I took a cleaver right down the middle, I'd have matching halves. That's very important."

Purple hair added, "You just need to learn to emphasize your bad features and hide your good ones."

"Other way around, Sarah."

"Oh. Oops."

"See?" she said, turning our faces back toward each other. "No need to be so sensitive. We're going to help you, and it's important for us girls to be honest with each other, don't you agree?"

My body was shivering, on fire with deep sexual feelings that had nowhere to go. Her fingers clutching my face and pinching my cheeks together were burning my skin to ash. I felt like she'd swallowed me whole and the walls of her stomach were crushing me.

She smiled at me with all her teeth and nodded my head for me.

* * *

"I thought we agreed we didn't want to do shit like this." My friend was watching me practice walking in heels, even though they made me so tall I could hit my head on the tops of door frames.

"Yeah well," I said as *her* words knocked through my head. *Weight on the balls of your feet. Heel then toe. Keep your shoulders back; you're not doing your tiny titties any favors when you slouch.* "It's nice to be feminine; what's wrong with that?"

My friend, Aisling, had her dark hair done up in a single three-strand braid. "We've talked about this. Heels change the shape of your spine, makeup removes perfectly normal 'flaws,' all of it—gah, you—you know exactly what I'm talking about."

"Well," I said, as the heel of my shoe hit the floor and then the toe. I was starting to get the hang of it. "It's easy for you to say. You pass without even having to try."

"Excuse me? It's not *privilege* to resist the patriarchy."

I shot back, "And it's not white supremacy to want to go shopping for groceries without getting misgendered."

An awkward quiet passed between us. "How is this going to help with that?" she asked, her voice soft in that way that told me in this moment, she felt small.

I was feeling small too. I was looking at myself in the floor-length mirror, looking at how my shoulders were almost twice as wide as my hips, at how I was so tall in these heels I could not even see the top of my head in the mirror. "I don't know. But you should see them, Ashy, you should see how pretty they are. And they think I can be like them."

"They're just using you. Bullying you. They're just those queersling types that get a sliver of acceptance and then turn around and use it to hurt their own kind." She sighed.

"Oh, so you think I can't pass?"

"I didn't say that." Her voice was soft around the edges, careful.

"What if they just want to help me?" I turned to look at her.

"Help you what? Become some bimbo?"

I gawked. "No!" I turned toward the mirror and said, "I'm done talking about this."

"Okay," she said. The room became suffocated with quiet for a long moment. "Those are nice-looking heels though," she admitted after a while.

"Thank you."

* * *

The next day I was in a coffee shop, and I was sitting on the couch waiting for my new friends to arrive.

When they came in, and I finally got a look at them, they were in much more casual clothing, wearing crop tops and jeans and warm-looking jackets. Except for *her*. *She* was in a short skirt and a sports bra, and her blonde hair was dripping around her shoulders like water from a melting glacier.

"Hi," I said, waving them over. They walked over with those perfect hip sways and arrayed themselves around the cozy corner with her immediately sliding toward the couch and then turning toward me, looking out at me from behind those shades.

"This is cute," she said. Her legs were spread just enough that I caught a glimpse of her panties.

I swallowed and looked away in the same instant. "Y-yeah. I mean, thanks."

"Girl, your *eyeliner*," came the voice of the redhead whose name I then knew as Kate.

I felt the brush of long nails as a cold hand wrapped its fingers around the back of my neck. A body next to me. I turned toward her and she was laying me out like meat on the slab.

"Classic baby tranny stuff here," she giggled, and I turned red. "You've left white spots closer to your eye."

"It's hard," I blurted. "I—"

"Shh," she said. I felt her hands on my shoulders pushing me down on the couch. "I'll fix it. Be still. Don't move a muscle." She threw her leg and straddled me like a pony and pulled out a liner pen that looked like it would poke a hole in my cornea. She did not move, even though she must have felt something pushing up at her from between my legs.

I looked around. The other coffee shop patrons, and the staff, were pointedly not looking at us. But my face flushed.

"I said don't move," came the voice in front of me.

I looked back at her.

"Keep your eyes on mine," she said. "Or I'll poke your eye out." A grin split her lips.

I could make out the blue of her irises from behind those shades. They were a dark blue, or maybe that was just the filter. I stared at them, transfixed by both their beauty and my fear. She took her pen and pointed it at my eye, and only a millimeter from pushing that sharp tip into the soft sack of water beneath, filled in the blank spots on my skin between where I'd done my liner and the red-streaked white my eyelids were supposed to protect. I was holding them pried open, swallowing fear, while someone I'd met only a few days ago threatened them with an ink-filled knife. It felt like a test.

"There," she finished. "Much better."

* * *

Later that day, Aisling and I were sitting in a quiet corner of the library, books from our chemistry class lay open on the table alongside a buffet of loose-leaf notes and flash cards.

"So do you all ever talk about anything besides sex and makeup?" Aisling whispered, her eyes searching to try and read the unwritten on my face.

I rolled my eyes into my materials. "Don't act like my makeup isn't on point today."

"It looks good. You look beautiful," Aisling said, "but like—the—I mean. Your new friends. Do they, does anyone talk besides her? Like can you describe their personalities? It sounds like they just. Sit around and insult you until she 'fixes' you."

"And the results speak for themselves."

"You were always beautiful," she said. "You know that right? You know you're perfect and special just the way you are?"

"Ashy, you know I love you. And your support has gotten me through a lot. The worst period of my life but," I sighed, "I know. I, but I don't want to just be a woman to myself. I want to be one to everyone, y'know? It's-it's not enough for me, I don't think. I, no matter what I do or say to affirm myself, I just see my mom's son in the mirror."

"Jules..." She walked around the table and squatted, putting her hands on my knees. "Jules, I know it's tough. I know. But—"

"You don't know," I shot back, a little louder than a whisper. "I'm sorry Ash, but you don't. It's..." I found myself crying, in spite of trying to hold back the tears. I lowered my voice again. "It's been so hard. Not passing. And... this hugboxing. It didn't help me get better."

"Better at what?"

"Better at being a woman. If—I'm sorry. If gender is a performance, then you can be good at it or bad at it. I'm bad at it."

"I'm bad at it too."

I shook my head. "It's not the same," I said. "It's not. You got good at being a woman and chose to perform it less. I never got good at it in the first place." I wiped my tears away with my arms. "It's just so hard to see myself as a woman when no one else sees me that way."

"*I* see you that way. That used to be enough." Her fingers squeezed my knees. "Fuck what society thinks; they're awful, Julie. They're awful."

Slowly, my hands reached over and curled their fingers around hers. "You're right," I whispered, my voice ragged around the edges.

"Enjoy your high femme friends, okay? I'm not saying you can't be friends with them." She gave my hands a squeeze. "Just, stay you, you know? The world, the world is a beautiful place because you're in it, and you're you. Okay?"

I looked up from my legs to her; my mascara and my eyeliner were, no doubt, running down my cheeks with my tears in little black rivers. "Okay," I said. "Thank you, Aisling. For being my friend."

"Thank *you* for being *my* friend."

* * *

A brush and a sponge. Two fingers. Three dispensers. Lotion.

Foundation on, then contour? Or contour, then foundation? No, no, no. It doesn't matter. Just the color blending matters. Get the eyeliner in. Get it in. No white space around the eyes. Good, good.

Damn these eyelids. They're so ugly, droopy, like a canopy over my eye. That's attractive. All the boys love a girl they can use as an umbrella. (Why am I thinking about boys? I don't even like boys.)

Fuck it, wipe it, start over. Fingers for foundation, blend, contour, blend with sponge, highlights, okay.

Is it happening? Don't bother with wing tips, amateur. Just get it done.

I looked up at myself in the mirror. It looked and felt like I was wearing a different face; my skin sparkled in the lights above my sink. My eyeshadow brought the dark colors out of my eyes. I fluttered my fake eyelashes. It looked good. But Aisling was right. It's not me. It's not even *beautiful*. I sighed. At least *she* will be impressed by my improvement. I hoped.

* * *

She'd asked to meet up at Flush again and said it'd just be the two of us. Before I walked in, I took out a mirror I'd brought and checked my makeup in the lights outside. Looks good, I hoped. *Not that it matters*, I thought, *because this will be the last time I wear this much makeup.* I had just wanted to show her I could do it before I decided I wouldn't. I walked in wearing my heels, perfect form, my hips swaying, what breasts I did have pushed up.

"Evening miss, ID please," came a voice to my right.

I turned to the guy, and he was looking at me. I actually turned around and looked *behind* me so I could see who he was talking to. I turned back to see him rolling his eyes and holding his hand out. I put my ID in it, got it back, and walked in.

The dance floor was illuminated. The crowd on it was spread out, encircling one particular dancer who stood in the center of the bar as a slow build of hard-bass electronic music played. Notes hit so loud and so deep they rattled the floor. The music was still just building, but she was hitting the air with her hips on the beat as if it were her hips that shook the ground instead of the music.

The floor flashed with her, painting the bar in colors in time with the music, dark ones, bright ones, blue, pink, white. I don't know if there actually was music playing or it was her body.

The drop came in. Her body moved with such grace and purpose, and the whole time she had a smile on her face. Her teeth flashed like blades in the club's lights. So cold they burned to the touch. She had all of our eyes stuck to her, to the way her body played the air, to the way she made the earth quake, the way she kicked up in the air and ran her fingers down her thighs, like she'd go further, but then striking the floor and shaking it.

Then her eyes met mine. I could feel her looking at me from behind her shades. I had ended up at the edge of the circle without even realizing I'd walked there. She beckoned to me with her fingers, and before I knew it, I felt my heels clicking on the floor. She pulled me into the center with all the people staring at us, and I stood there embarrassed. They could see my shoulders, my height, the hips I could not shake because I didn't really have any. I felt myself shrink into my own body in an impossible attempt to make me invisible. Then, an open hand struck me like thunder from a black sky, and I looked up in shock as pain exploded across my skin.

She was there, wagging her finger in my face like she was my mother; she stood there for a moment just hitting the air with her hips to the beat, and she looked at me over the top of her glasses. I still couldn't make out the color, but I felt like a thief locked in the stockades, gawked at by the public.

She pointed at my hips and then at her own. I began to shake mine to the beat, while she danced around me in a slow circle, stopping once to show me one step, and then another. Simple steps: nothing like what she was doing. But I began to feel an ecstasy enter my body. They were looking at *us*, not just her, *us*. Me. They were all looking at me. Was I beautiful?

I turned my eyes from the crowd back to her. She was smiling, more widely than I've ever seen anyone smile. She was staring at me like she knew what I was thinking.

I was thinking, "*Am I beautiful?*"

* * *

She pushed me against the door to my room. She placed her hand on the doorframe beside me, blocking me in. She looked up at me with a toothy grin, and her finger traced the bone between my breasts up and down. "Your makeup looks good."

I blushed. "Thank you."

She turned the handle of my door and it fell away behind me. *Did I even unlock it?* I thought as I stumbled inside, and she shoved me in further. Desire was consuming my body, but I was holding it down as best as I could.

"Wait," I said. "There's—there's something I need to say."

"Oh?" She tilted her head at me, her shades glistening at the darkness of my entrance. As she walked in after me, I felt like I was being hunted.

"Yes, I appreciate all your advice." I stood up straight and took a deep breath. "But all this advice, you're just trying to turn me into you. And I can't be you, I'll never be as good at being you as you are. But I can be the best at being me."

She paused, half covered in the shadows, but I could tell she tilted her head by the way the light on her sunglasses shifted. "Well," she said, her voice a low growl that reached through the air like the webs of a spider, "today kids, we've learned about the importance of being yourself."

My blood ran cold. I felt like my heart stopped.

She kept walking toward me. She emerged into the light, her smile unbroken. Wider, even. Like I was struggling in her web, and it was only making her salivate even more. "Sit," she said, pointing at the ground.

I did so.

She put her heel on my face and shoved me back onto my floor. I lay there, staring at my ceiling with wide eyes as I heard her shuffle her shoes off her feet and felt her toes spreading my legs to make a place for herself. She crawled up between them, her hands on either side of my stomach and then on my shoulders when she could finally look down at me.

Then, in one fluid motion, she pulled off her sunglasses. I could finally see into her eyes, and they were blue, but not the kind of blue I'd ever seen on a human face before. It was like staring at the bottom of a glacier from the top of it. I could see straight down through the ice into the darkness below.

"Look at you." Her fingernails were tapping on the side of

my throat. "So ashamed of your own desires. You want these things." She traced the side of my ear with the sharp end of her nail. "Of course you do, but you're not supposed to want things, are you?" She bent over and whispered in my ear, her breath stealing the heat from my skin as if she were the waving waters of Lake Superior herself. "Good girls don't want things. Good girls learn to be happy with what they have." Her legs squeezed my hips, and the places our bodies met heated. "Don't worry." Her tongue snuck out to lick her teeth. "You don't have to want things anymore." Her pale blue eyes nailed mine to the floor. "I'll give them to you anyway."

I swallowed, dryly. I nodded.

"Good girl."

* * *

Aisling and I met in a coffee shop for our study session. My hair was draped around my shoulders and pinned up behind my ears with sparkling hair clips. My nails were long and pink, with little sparkling jewels glued in the center of each one. I decided to go with a bit of a pink motif across the board. Pink lips, pink eyeshadow with a little gold at the edges of it. Black eyeliner, of course, can't get too ambitious yet. A nice bright pink blush with a streak of glittery highlight, kind of subtle so that it only really shows when it catches a light.

When she walked in, I was already sitting at a table. My eyes flicked up from my work to her. She stopped and stared at me for a moment, before slowly making her way to a seat.

"I almost didn't recognize you," she said.

I couldn't help but preen. "Thank you."

She nodded. She looked at me for a long time. "So, you like this."

"Yes," I said, managing to only sound a little offended.

"You wore all that just to come study and get coffee?"

I tilted my head. "Why not?"

"I mean," she said, speaking like she was trying to tiptoe across a creaky floor, "if it makes you happy."

"Good to know I have your permission," I said.

She looked at me askance but said nothing, just cracked open her chemistry book. I cracked open mine and got my laptop out, and it was difficult to type with the long nails, and I was not practiced at working around them. It noticeably slowed my typing. When I looked up, Aisling was looking at my nails on my keyboard, and then up at me.

"You got a problem?" I asked.

She flinched. Was I louder than I meant to be? "You— what you just said—I feel very uncomfortable, Jules. You're, are you feeling all right?"

"I'm perfectly fine," I said, wiggling my shoulders in my dress. "I just don't like being judged is all."

She stared at me for the longest time, and I pointedly ignored her. "Jules," she began, softly, "if, please just listen. If you really like being like this, if this is who you are, I'll support you one hundred percent. But if you don't like this, if something's wrong, please, I-I need you to tell me. I just want to help."

"Nothing's wrong!" My words drew across my throat like a bow pressed too hard to its violin. "This is just who I am. And I love it. I love who I am now. You-you're just jealous because I'm pretty, and you're not."

The words struck her like a hammer on a bell, and I watched her crack from her bottom all the way to her top. She stood up, tears coming to her eyes. "Well," she said, "I hope. You're telling the truth. I hope you're happy now. For your sake." She quickly started shoving all of her study materials into her bag, bending and crumpling papers, crushing them under the books, and then turned and left.

I watched her go, my heart sinking out of my chest and onto the floor. *How could I say that to her?* I thought. But the worst part was I noticed a thrill climbing up my chest. A rush of power. I had turned her into crying mush with just a few words. I felt *powerful*.

I recoiled at this part of myself. All those people, those girls, those boys, who had shoved me around in high school to make themselves feel big because they *sensed* I was different before *I* even knew. I was just like them. I had become just like them.

I looked down at my pink nails with new eyes, and they seemed less like ornaments and more like claws. I raised them in front of my face, turning them back and forth. I had used my tongue like a weapon, and I had cut the person who supported me when everyone else had abandoned me, and all because I had achieved just a sliver, just a taste of acceptance.

My hands shook with the horror I was feeling, and I reached down and began breaking my nails against the table, one by one. I pulled a wipe out of my bag, and I wiped my face with it. I kicked off my shoes in the middle of the coffee shop. I stood up, barefoot, shoved my study materials into my bag, and walked out. I didn't care who was staring, this had to come to an end, and I knew exactly where to go next to end it.

* * *

I showed up at her door, my face set in determination. When she opened the door, her sunglasses were gone, and those abyssal blue eyes stared back at me. The look on my face did not seem to budge her. The smile on her face was toothless.

"Come in," she said. "It's right this way."

I followed her, replying, "Actually I wanted to talk to you."

"Oh?" she said, sounding almost bored. She walked over to the other side of her living room, down to a little white-walled hallway that led to a wooden bedroom door.

"Yeah. I think I've changed my mind," I said as I followed her to the end of that hallway.

She turned the handle. "Is that so?" she responded, dispassionately.

I nodded as the door swung open into a long corridor, too dark to see the other side of. I could tell the walls were made of stone. Little gray rocks piled on top of each other, held together with packed earth.

She started down the hallway, and I followed her. "Tell me about it."

"This thing we're doing, it's, I know you want to help me and your intentions are good."

"Mhm."

"But it's not me," I said as we made our way down the long dark corridor. It seemed impossibly long. "And I think-I think I need to find a way to be that suits me, y'know? Not weighed down by like, beauty standards and stuff like that."

She was no longer responding, and the paved stone floors became dirt, which became grass. The walls faded away into the darkness as if they were never there, and the stars of the night sky burnished a void sliced in twain by the Milky Way. These lights in the darkness stared down at us through gnarled branches, charred black and twisting over us like teeth. I passed through them, through an archway of these branches until we emerged into a clearing, where the moon sat framed by mountainous ridges in the distance: perfectly cradled by the shadow of the earth. I stood there, the three other girls standing there already. The two in the back, their red and purple hair gleaming in the moonlight, stood naked in the glaring darkness, standing in the water up to their knees. They mirrored each other, their palms pressed together in front of their chests, between their breasts. The third stood between them, directly beneath the moon, her feet buried halfway up her ankle in the sand.

She stood at the edge of the clearing, removing her clothes.

I followed suit and said, "What I'm saying is I don't want to do this anymore. The answer is no. I want to stay me, for better or worse."

Naked and beautiful as a gust of snow on a frozen lake, she walked past them and stood between the back two at the edge of the water. Then she took one step on it, and it turned to ice beneath her feet, spiraling outward in patterns too complex for my eye to process. In staring at them, I felt the madness of contemplating the impossible begin to scratch at the edges of my eyes. I looked at her instead, every contour of her body carved from rock older even than the planet she stood on. The sight of her as she walked out on the surface of the lake she'd frozen filled me with such powerful and intense sexual pleasure that I collapsed to my knees on the spot. My lips trembled. I could not look away from her as she turned toward us. Her ankles together, she reached up and cradled the very moon between her hands, her fingers sliding alongside the silhouette of the mountains.

At this, the girls whose legs had become stuck in the ice of the lake began contorting their bodies with the sickening snap of bone. Their heads twisted, their arms snapped and bent in four different places as they too reached for the moon, their fingers cutting through the air like the gnarled branches of the trees behind me. The one with her feet in the sand bent too, her legs bending twice the wrong way with two loud snaps. Her body was suspended, bent forward and then backward over the sand, as she extended her arms out away from her sides in the same gnarled way. Her contortion ended when her legs were spread, her body lay across the ground, her head half sunken into the ice, and her hair woven through its surface in those same unreadable patterns.

As I made my way to her and began to use her as a bridge to cross from the land to the ice, I felt with my feet an expression on her face that shouted a feeling there were no words for. As I felt the contours of the ice in my feet, I felt I was standing on a language that would slice my tongue if I tried to speak it. I walked in a straight line between the two gnarled bodies I had just yesterday called my friends. Somewhere in between stepping on the ice and making it halfway toward *her*, my eyes had been drawn from her to the moon.

I don't want to do this. Don't make me do this, I thought at her. I could no longer open my lips to speak. I could see out of the corner of my eye that she was just staring at me. I could see in those two deep lakes of blue that she knew, and I knew, that she would never and had never made me do anything. I chose this.

I chose this and with every step, I was choosing it again.

No, I thought. But then I stood before her, and she took her hands off the moon to put them on either side of my face. Hunger in her teeth. She pushed down on me, and I felt myself pass through the ice as if it were opening up to grab me, to wrap me. I was rattling on the inside, but my body did not shake. It was pinned in place, but I felt myself on the edge of orgasm, if I could have moved my body to allow my muscles to spasm, to work out the feelings, it would have given me some relief, but instead, I was suffocating as if I had been vacuum sealed in a bag of stars and ice and darkness and the most beautiful thing I had never seen. When my penis passed into the ice, the sensation became so strong I felt like it would kill me. My thoughts disappeared; I could not even control that anymore. It was just that one singular feeling, sharp as a pin but broad as a sunless sea.

It was only when my head, the last thing to be swallowed, was finally consumed, and I got my last look up through the intricate swirls of that ice, the shadow of the moon looming over me as if it were only miles away, that I was overwhelmed by an orgasm so strong that it blacked out my vision, and I felt myself slip from ice into a deep and liquid void.

* * *

I have memories. Memories of being insecure, of feeling powerless, of feeling ugly. Memories of being a man, if I dig back far enough. But when I walk into the bookstore, the cold comes in with me. I slice through the warmth like a knife. I take a bite out of the peach in my hand. The fuzz tickles my plump, flushed lips, and the sweet juices come into my mouth and gently drip down my chin.

My icy blue eyes scan the store, and they spot a girl on one of the soft seats, reading. She is slouched over, wearing a sweater that's too big for her, and a choker to try and hide her Adam's apple. Her eyes catch my breasts first, and then my face, and then she quickly looks away. My sunglasses with pink rims mean she can't be sure I caught her looking.

My tongue licks the sweetness out of the peach where my teeth tore it open, and my heels click the floor, and my hips sway, and I walk toward her as if the whole world belonged to me.

I stand over her, taking another bite out of my peach. She looks up at me.

"Whatcha readin'?"

* * *

Discussion Questions

1. How would you describe the personality of the antagonist/love interest in the story? What are her motivations? Does a person have to be perfect to be "good"?

2. The narrator says, "If gender is a performance, then you can be good at it or bad at it." What does this statement mean, and do you agree with it? Is it wrong for the narrator to want to be good at the performance of being a woman? Is it wrong for a woman to want to be good at the performance of being a woman?

3. Can the narrator be a trans woman without being girly? Or does the very act of being a trans woman require it?

4. How is the narrator improving her makeup to be more desirable to her love interest any different than women shaving their legs and underarms to be more desirable to men? (*Or men shaving their chest hair?*)

5. What does the narrator want: To be beautiful to others? To be accepted as a woman by others? To be powerful and important in the eyes of others? Or something else? What advice would you give her about her desires?

* * *

Freeing Free Will

Matthew Thomas Bernell

* * *

<u>**Content Disclosure**</u>: Strong Language

* * *

Sloan ran their stubby fingers through their tight curls and lay in the cool leather chair. Dr. Dinet, their psychiatrist, was tapping a pencil on a clipboard, waiting for a response. The impatience wasn't entirely undue. This had been Sloan's fourth appointment in just two months, and they had failed to make a decision about the medication. Instead, they seemed to spend the appointment bringing up a problem from the familiar set of personal and mental problems they always brought up, only to let their eyes wander to the shipwreck memorabilia on Dr. Dinet's walls, which told the history of the Titanic's doomed voyage via newspaper clippings, magazines, framed photos, and even a boat wheel. Sloan wondered if this was appropriate for the setting, given the slew of depressives Dr. Dinet saw each day. They recollected a fishing trip with their father when they were young, how the boat had not been plugged up correctly and began taking on water, their father bailing out the boat by hand while shouting for help. The help did eventually come, but they never went out on that boat again together.

Dr. Dinet kept tapping the pencil, though not too forcefully. In fact, it might have been primarily boredom mixed with just a hint of impatience. This was what Sloan told themself when they snapped out of the daydream.

"Sloan, I don't want to pressure you. It *is* experimental. Studies show, however, no side effects other than mild nausea. Based on what you're telling me, it seems like the best treatment, but I know this decision has troubled you. Would you like to discuss it further? I won't prescribe it if you don't think it's best."

Sloan straightened themself up and brushed their hands along a purple flannel shirt still damp from the drizzle on the way in. They crinkled their nose and tightened the muscles of their pale face in a way that suggested inner conflict, and then they ran their thumb and forefinger along the bridge of their nose in an attempt to alleviate said conflict. Then, they replied, "Okay, the issue is that... well, I don't want to *have* to take the medicine, but I want what the medicine will provide. I want to want the medicine, but I'm just struggling with willing myself to say yes because... I don't know. Is it crazy to think imperfection is fine?" They huffed faintly as they said this.

Dr. Dinet nodded understandingly. "No, Sloan, I don't think that's crazy at all, and you know I don't like when you use that word."

Sloan rolled their large hazel eyes and softly said, "Yeah, sorry."

"The goal isn't to eliminate imperfection. No one will ever be perfect. The goal is simply to allow you to act how you truly want to act. For example, your complaints over the last two years since your mother died have been primarily volitional in nature. You are eating more than you want to eat, feel like you can't stop, not exercising even though you love exercise. You said in our last session that you have wanted to learn an instrument, even bought a guitar, but it has sat on its stand in your room because, quote, 'I just can't direct my energies toward anything really meaningful.' Volitor will not eliminate your desires. It won't change who you are as the complex person you are. It simply will, if successful, allow you to act the way you want to act."

Something clicked inside of Sloan. They audibly attempted to swallow despite their dry mouth and said, "Okay. I want to see what it's like at least."

Dr. Dinet explained how the dosages would start small and titrate up, that it was still uncertain if the medicine would need to be taken forever or if it were possible to wean off and, perhaps, to achieve greater autonomy through a kind of habituation to such autonomy being the standard mode of operation.

As they exited the office, Sloan checked Twitter and all three Gmail accounts before walking through the doors, and upon walking out into the world, noticed the rain had subsided. There was a crabapple tree glazed with rain beside the office, and they stood briefly to admire the depth of the green of its leaves as finches played in its wiry branches, their world one of so many leaps and plunges. Sloan walked back to their car hoping that such attentiveness to the small beauties of the world around them would not be such a rare occurrence once the Volitor had taken effect.

* * *

Sloan had not yet told anyone about their decision. It was a private matter, and they didn't want to be judged negatively. If they were to gain willpower, they wanted others to see them as the possessor of such willpower, not as a sick person in need of treatment. They arrived at their apartment after stopping by the pharmacy and greeted Zander upon arrival. Zander was lounging on the couch watching an adult cartoon while ripping a bong. It was a familiar scene. Sloan took part sometimes, but there had been a freakout a few months back, an ice bath and hyperventilation and Zander promising over and over again in their raspy low voice that it wasn't a heart attack. It wasn't. Still, it soured the experience and Sloan had not partaken since.

The roommates exchanged greetings. Sloan said they were going to make dinner later if Zander cleaned. This, too, was common, and equally common that Zander would not, in fact, clean, at least not without extra prodding. At this point, Sloan had decided and kept secret that they would not be asking to renew the lease with Zander, so they had made peace with the extra labor. It did feel like a heavy burden though, as if coming home were another sort of work, a job where social media needed to be tended, after-hours emails responded to, meals cooked, dishes cleaned, instruments learned, entertainment consumed, bathing, hair care. Sloan went right to their room after the exchange of greetings, opened the Volitor package, and gave themself the shot. It was practically painless, and the world did not immediately transform from the sloppy and disorganized mess of impulses and commands that they had become familiar with. Everything seemed completely normal.

Sloan went to the kitchen and began dicing onion and

garlic. They decided to make a roux and prepare homemade mac and cheese. It was a recipe taught to them by their mother. It wasn't the kind of thing they had learned in a single lesson, but rather the sort of thing instilled in them as if a virtue, a habit built up over regularly preparing the meal on Thursdays after their brother had come home from his weekly football game. The first time their mother had left them in charge, the roux had failed miserably and become a kind of clumpy gravy and the faces of all the family members reflected this failure. This iteration was a success, creamy and delicate, the pasta with just the right bite, finished with sprinkles of chives and a little pink salt. Zander was greatly appreciative of this, scarfing the bowl down quickly, ravenously in their red-eyed zombified hunger. They did manage a "thank you," but Sloan took care of the dishes and said not to worry about it this time. They had eaten most of their bowl but didn't feel the need to go back for seconds. It was a good, simple meal.

It was only eight p.m. when the dishes were done and put away. A rainy Saturday often meant about six hours of doomscrolling under a quilt their grandmother had sewn almost half a century prior, a couple hours of chores and cooking, often less, the remainder spent on TV and a nap. This had been the custom since their mother's death, though it had certainly not been uncommon previously. Tonight, though, Sloan sat at their desk and found a tutorial on YouTube where a chunky man with a funny hat claimed he could teach his followers to learn all the basic chords in only two weeks. Sloan picked up the guitar and used their flannel to wipe away some of the dust accumulated under the strings. They stretched their pudgy, soft hands, cracked their knuckles, and pressed play.

As they lay in bed that night, they checked their socials and realized they had twenty unread notifications. They felt a swelling of surprise upon seeing the red number on the screen. They had rarely accumulated so many without clearing them, the last time being at the hands of an overnight barrage of anger directed at Sloan over their endorsement of an unpopular political candidate. Sloan didn't think too long about anything that night. They felt content and scrolled a little past their normal bedtime, joking to themself the medicine must not be that good. Then they slept well.

* * *

After a year on Volitor, Sloan hardly resembled that earlier, more imperfect iteration of themself. They had lost weight, taken up running (to the astonishment of friends and their dad), and carried themself with shoulders held higher, chest extended but not absurdly so. Nonetheless, the change had nothing to do with style. Sloan still dressed like a dead rockstar from the nineties, still listened to the music of such rockstars, and they had been spending some of their savings on a black and gray sleeve of tattoos in the traditional style: peonies, a chef's knife, an old school heart with a cherub, a spiderweb on their elbow. And the surrounding cast had changed as well. Sloan had realized they did not really want to hang around Zander or most of that friend group. They had a studio apartment to themself downtown now, and they had found some friends through mutual hobbies, one friend, Sara, with whom they ran, and another, Brey, with whom they had been playing music on Sundays in Brey's basement. It was a musty, small basement, but fine, arguably perfectly suited, for the duo's spare indie rock.

Sloan had been considering stopping Volitor for some time now, as the effects had begun to feel deeply engrained, as if arising from within themself organically. They had almost come to long for the difficulty of dedication too. Life still had difficulties: the dishes, a rough patch at work a month ago, their father struggling with a new addiction to painkillers after a bout with back problems and lingering grief, Philly the tabby cat had escaped and nearly been run over by a station wagon. Ultimately, however, these were outside of Sloan's control, and they knew this. Nonetheless, they had seemed to become the version of themself that they truly wanted to be: active, creative, attentive, and focused. Even their mood disorder had become much more manageable because reactions to outside stimuli were controlled by a strong sense of internal reasoning. Feelings could be felt, but they rarely, if ever, were the basis for Sloan's will anymore.

Thus, Sloan arrived at Dr. Dinet's office for the first time in three months, the mists of September again dampening their outfit, the crabapple tree again glazed with rainwater, sheltering the busy finches. Their meetings had been set at quarterly intervals for the last six months, this being the second of them. Since the appointment in which Dr. Dinet prescribed Volitor, the emotional progress had been clear to both parties at each step of the way, resulting in less frequent meetings.

Dr. Dinet was looking different herself. She had a more well-kept appearance, and the office had become notably tidier over the last year. In the world around them, this seemed to be the trend for everything and everyone. People were losing weight; lines at drive-throughs were vacant. Some chains had shuttered. Certain sectors of the economy, specifically those concerning vice, had begun, over the last several months, a kind of free fall. Las Vegas was dropping prices across the board. Ads on Google advertised fifty-dollar flights and hundred-dollar weekend stays. The sports betting apps that had popped up like a ubiquitous social fungus over the previous five years had begun disappearing. Places of worship had increased attendance, as had universities, doctor offices, gyms, museums, and national parks. With this socioeconomic backdrop, it made sense to Sloan why the office was busy today, albeit orderly, as well as why Dr. Dinet had not been tapping the pencil while waiting for a response.

Sloan had dazed out again as still happened when they were in deep thought. Dr. Dinet was calm and had a caring, warm look in her eye, not a single hint of the prior impatience. She repeated the question: "Sloan, our new studies show that weaning off Volitor often results in a slight relapse of volitional alignment, but with at least a year of assisted habit-building, folks do tend to maintain the majority of the changes. There have been some cases of full relapse, though, and I want you to be aware of that."

Sloan had become accustomed to this sort of language. "Volitional alignment" had popped into cultural consciousness the way the jingle for Pepto had. It was simply how people spoke of Volitor and its effects. They had thought about this conversation enough and knew what they wanted. Sloan thanked the doctor for supporting their journey with Volitor, but they would like to go off. Dr. Dinet had no objections, and Sloan left the maritime tragedy-decorated office with a sense of optimism about this decision, anticipating a sense of difficulty in managing priorities again, the feeling of empowerment at overcoming an "unaligned volition" rather than making such things disappear chemically. Despite this, they feared the remainder of their Saturday. They were going to see their father who was living a bare-bones life in squalor, nursing a bad back and a new addiction to one of the oldest remedies for misery.

Their father had sold the family house after the death of his wife. He had not coped well and showed this in his haggard appearance, dirty nails, a voice filled with more gravel than ever before. He'd been let go from his longtime carpentry job and was coasting on gig work as a handyman. Walking into their father's apartment, Sloan instinctively looked at the wall-mounted pike covered in dust and gunk. In better times, their father had always kept this prized item clean. Sloan remembered the bragging their father would do when friends were invited over for small dinner parties, how he would end the story by saying it was actually the second-biggest fish he caught that day on Mille Lacs, would hold out his muscular tan arms to show the length of the one that got away, would join his fists together and rip them apart, wince and say, "Damn broken line." That man seemed long gone, but their father was asleep in his chair, snoring loudly.

"Dad, Dad!" Sloan called, putting a hand to the old man's shoulder. He was often hard to wake these days.

The old man jolted awake, spittle running down his beard onto the rough skin of his chest that bore an old tattoo, all of which had faded to a blue-gray mess. "Sloan! Oh..." he said in a tone caught between relief and disbelief that it was not yet the reaper.

"What are you doing? It's four p.m.," Sloan said somewhat sharply. They tried not to seem too critical, as he tended to have bad reactions to criticism, something that had been passed down to Sloan as well, though this had also been alleviated by Volitor.

"It's just an afternoon nap, Sloan. Ain't you had one of those before?" the old man said, raising himself up from the worn cloth of the chair. He went to the nearby kitchen and poured himself a glass of soda and drank it crudely, gulping loudly. "Did you come from your appointment?"

"Yes, Dad. It went well. I've decided to go off Volitor." Sloan had confided in their father about their Volitor use. He was the one person who knew, though others had, of course, assumed, given the drug's popularity. Even though the drug had simply become "what one does," it was still taboo to state that one was doing it, so as not to diminish the sense of accomplishment. Sloan had needed to tell someone. It had had such a profound impact that it couldn't be left fully undisclosed.

"Damn good choice if you ask me. All these people out here thinking they're missin' aligned or whatever you all say. I say it's the easy way out." He said this in his crotchety way, the gravel working its course along his vocal cords.

"You know I'm going to ask you to go on it again, Dad. I'm so tired of seeing you like this." Sloan motioned around at the filthy apartment. Clothes were piled on the floor, pill bottles and cigarette butts littered about, the filth accumulating around like the hoard of a dragon whose name was Regret or Helplessness.

"Get out of here with that. I'm free to do as I please, more than I can say for you all. You all think you're free and too good for being. I may not be as clean and proper but at least I do the work myself."

Sloan could sense the conversation was slipping and he'd be on one of his diatribes if they didn't correct course. "Okay,

okay. I just worry. Listen, I brought you some soup. Can I help clean up?" This was offered sincerely and sweetly.

The old man snorted dryly and wriggled his face, leaning against the wood countertop. "Yeah, all right I suppose." He was grateful. Sloan knew it. He didn't like to show gratitude though.

As the old man slurped some soup and watched college football, Sloan cleaned the dishes and put clothes in the washer that took up an unfortunate amount of space in the already cramped bathroom. When he had finished the soup, the old man began to put his dishes away and took to tidying up things himself in the living room. Sloan knew he was not an inherently lazy man, and this was one reason they didn't mind helping; it felt rational to help him in such a hard time, to preserve the ideally irrevocable bond of kinship. Sloan was thinking about this as they wiped down the key lime-green bathroom sink and the medicine cabinet that had popped open.

Sloan raised their gaze from the sink to the cabinet, reached to shut it, and saw there was a half-empty packet of Volitor staring right back at Sloan. They stood in the silence and stillness of disbelief, blinking slowly.

Sloan wasn't quick to react to the stimulus; there were many feelings. Confusion and anger and sadness and worry all blended together in some kind of emotional salad, each retaining their unique character while contributing to the feeling as a whole. They had always prized honesty and still did, so they took the packet and confronted their father, who did not immediately respond but went and sat back in the worn-out old chair.

"It doesn't work," he said, somber, suddenly sober, serious.

"What do you mean it doesn't work? The studies say…"

"The studies say fuck all, Sloan. Aligning the volitions or whatever don't do shit if they already are aligned."

"But, but…" Sloan couldn't understand. How could anyone want to live like this? It occurred to Sloan that their father simply had given up and had made the choice to do so. They had never doubted his love for their mother, his sincerity as he kept a smile every day through the treatments, never showing a sign of weakness, how he had shaved his own head and worn pink every day to his construction job. Sloan figured there must be an infinite chain of "want to's"—want to get better, want to want to get better, want to want to want to get better— and at some point, for their father, this chain might indeed terminate in a "get better," but that chain must have gone beyond the scope of Volitor.

"I want to want this life as it stands. I don't want much more. The doctors put me on the medicine, mandated it, and I figured 'what the hell,' but it didn't change much. I started calling you more often, yeah, because you know I want to want to be a good father, but I don't want to want to keep going much longer. Don't feel I was meant for a world without your mother."

Sloan had approached him and stood before him now. He put his head against Sloan's damp wool zip-up, wrapped his arms around them, and wept. Sloan stopped thinking about what their father wanted in the grand scheme of things and focused on what he wanted right now. They leaned down and put their arms around the old man, felt him trembling, and they knew then that in any possible world they would have wanted this man as a father, that he was fundamentally good and they would choose him regardless of his habits. In the tightness of their embrace, Sloan felt grateful for the world that had given them such a father, though they remained silent, as if in prayer.

* * *

Discussion Questions

1. Volitor helps provide people with the motivation to do the things they want to be doing. Is human value based on getting things done or being the kind of person that gets things done? Does it matter?

2. What do you think are the causes of people not doing the things they want to do? How do you know if failing to do the things you want is a good thing or a bad thing? Or is it always a bad thing?

3. What do you think culture, and the world, would look like if everyone was on Volitor? Would humanity be better or worse? If you were to take Volitor, how would your life change? What keeps you from doing those things now?

4. The new Sloan ended up with all new friends once they started taking Volitor. Do you think in real life that is typically the case? Are your friends holding you back, or is it something else?

5. Sloan's gender is unclear in the story. Did you imagine Sloan's gender? If so, what did you imagine? How/why might your understanding of the story change if you had known Sloan were female? If Sloan were male? If Sloan were nonbinary?

* * *

Shepherds

Aweed Nyoka

* * *

Content Disclosure: Mild Violence

* * *

The small vessel descended swiftly through the atmosphere. Beneath the clouds, a deep blue ocean gave way to a gray shoreline typical of cultures at this developmental stage. The dominant species on this planet was building. Not toward any goal in particular. Just testing the limits of their environment, like small children. Thriving might come later. First, the species had to overcome its youth. This is why the Shepherds had come. To provide the structure every child needs to survive.

Explosions colored the viewing window all shades of red, orange, and black. Metallic dings echoed off the vessel's hard exterior. The junior Shepherd had seen landing videos but still jumped at the abrupt cacophony. Deftly maneuvering for landing, Senior extended a sense tendril in reassurance. Junior took it in her own, allowing the moderating energy to flow through her. It was an act of trust, merging one's feelings with another. Despite their disparity in rank, there was no hierarchy in this gesture. Her respect for Senior grew.

They touched down amid the dense, colored fog. The canopy opened and the Shepherds stepped out, dauntless, to the ground. Junior mirrored Senior, standing still as munitions detonated against or glanced off their personal shields. She recalled her training. *They will fear you. Do not take it personally. We have made contact in every way possible, but the response is always the same. They have fancied themselves gods for so long, and will not release that fantasy easily.*

Still, she felt sad. Although she could see no one through the storm of projectiles, their collective fear assaulted her senses, thicker than the smoke and fire. She winced. Junior had never felt that afraid. She would not know what to do if she did. Eventually, the roaring flashes faded. The air cleared. The Shepherds stood before their vessel, surrounded completely by machines of war. Tall buildings towered beyond. One stood closest, separated from the rest by a lifeless waterway. Vibrant flags of many colors and symbols rippled in the wind. Blue script on a large sign read: United Nations.

Senior activated her translator and spoke. "We apologize for arriving unannounced. We have no weapons and wish only to speak with your representatives. Please." After a long pause, several war machines rolled aside to allow a delegation through. Five humans wrapped in dark cloth walked forward. They were flanked by a dozen more in dark armor. The whole procession wobbled into the shadows of the much larger Shepherds. Already severely limited on only two fleshy legs, they had to navigate smoking craters and charred corpses of their own making. Their movement was physically awkward, and every face betrayed psychological humiliation as well. Junior knew human anatomy from her research. Over millions of years, they willed their bodies and sense organs to shrivel in favor of more complex brains, congratulating themselves for mentally overpowering their stronger and more attuned neighbors. Now they looked up at the visitors with ocular organs that perceived only a sliver of the electromagnetic spectrum. Junior could feel their hormones surging within and between their bodies, causing them to feel everything but comprehend little. They smelled like death, uncaring of the animals wrapped around their waists, covering their feet, and moving through their digestive tracts.

The delegation stopped several human body lengths away. One of the unarmored humans raised a conical device to their mouthparts and spoke. "You asked for a representative. I am the democratically elected leader of the most powerful nation on Earth. I represent its interests." He spoke the last word with strange emphasis. Something approaching hunger.

Junior's research on the dominant human culture of this planet was extensive. Even so, she did not really believe until this moment that one person would claim full diplomatic power over a species of billions, let alone millions of other species.

The human gestured with an upper leg to his four colleagues. "We are the United Nations Security Council, the highest decision-making body of our people. But you already know that, having landed just outside our international headquarters on one of the rare occasions that each of us is present."

"Yes," Senior replied with a bow of her head to show

respect in a common, terrestrial fashion.

"And am I also correct in assuming you have some motive beyond our complete destruction, given that you have not deployed your clearly superior technology against us, even after we deployed ours against you?"

"Yes."

The president did not confer with his colleagues, and no one challenged his authority to speak on their behalf. Junior's research again failed to preempt her surprise at human society. Theirs was a powerfully entrenched dictatorship, barely disguised.

"All right. You say you wish only to speak. What have you come to say?"

The president's ingratitude frustrated Junior. Without warning or restraint, they had tried to kill the only life they had ever encountered from beyond their world. When they failed, there was no apology. No attempt at reconciliation. Just embarrassment thinly masked as brusque bravado. Perhaps the Academy was right, Junior thought. These people really did need to be protected from themselves.

Senior responded calmly. "We offer more."

"More of what?" the president demanded.

Senior tilted her head toward the human bodies smoldering around them, though most were unrecognizable. The delegation did not need to know her ocular organs were located far from her head. "More than this."

The president breathed through his mouth parts in anger, and Junior could feel his blood pressure rising. "Did you come all the way from wherever you came from just to insult us?"

"No."

"Then why? What do you mean by *more*? More resources? Technology? Spaceships and shields like yours?"

"Yes."

A murmur drifted through the crowd that was rapidly gathering just beyond a makeshift perimeter. Humans were pointing personal screens at Junior and Senior, verbally describing the scene as if for listeners elsewhere. At first, the armored humans fired their handheld weapons into the contracting crowd to nonlethal—though clearly painful—effect. But there was far too much curiosity. Spectating humans overwhelmed the numerically inferior militants, flowing past them and crawling atop war machines for a chance to see the Shepherds. Small, flying machines hovered above with little lenses and screens of their own.

The president finally turned to confer with the rest of the Security Council. There was much nodding and nervous excitement. Junior could see Senior's basic formula would work as it had on a thousand other worlds. Before the president turned to respond, someone from the crowd shouted, "Yeah, and what'll it cost us?" The human was quickly and roughly removed from view by several armored guards.

Senior answered the question anyway. "A gift costs nothing." Louder murmurs now.

The president glared at the spot from which the apparently unauthorized human had shouted, clearly offended at any interruption. He attempted to regain control with a casual tone. "We have a saying where I come from. There's no such thing as a free lunch. What do you gain by coming here?"

Senior nodded. "Allies."

"Against what?"

"You will not understand. If they found you first, you would not know it. You would simply cease to exist. But we found you first. You seek the stars. We can give them to you."

The crowd erupted into a din, quieting to hear Senior's reply only after the president bellowed into his voice projector. "And what would you ask of your new allies in return for the stars?"

Senior's own voice remained as warm and authoritative as ever. "Nothing in your lifetimes. You have much to learn before you can even protect yourselves. And much more before you can assist others."

Someone from the crowd shouted at the president. "What are you waiting for? Think you'll get reelected if they get tired of your questions and leave us alone on this rock?"

That did it, Junior knew. Nothing mattered more to this man than power. Power was the foundation of their whole culture. Perhaps of every culture on the cusp of solar expansion. The power to overcome all competitors within and outside their species. What else, then, but the stars and all else that might be overcome? They would accept the gift. They would escape as they intended. And they would never ask why the gift was necessary. They would not see that without guidance, they would never achieve their goal. They would exhaust the means to escape too soon. They would die trying. For the first time, Junior wondered if her own culture was so different once. They could not have always been Shepherds.

Junior was shaken from her thoughts by the president's newly boisterous tone. "So what do we do, shake hands? I don't want to lose one of mine in front of all these fine people." He grinned widely, sweeping an arm toward the crowd and their multitude of recording devices. He clearly understood the immortality he was claiming by single-handedly brokering the first extraterrestrial alliance in sanctioned human history. Junior thought it was unfortunate that such a profoundly unpleasant creature should be the one to receive that distinction. His crude comment insulted the graceful curve of the Shepherds' leg scythes by suggesting they were used for violence rather than cultivating food. That an elder like Senior could sharpen and blunt her scythes to suit her situation, he could not know, of course, but he did not care to know either, and that meant everything.

"Unnecessary. Materials will arrive soon." Senior had performed marvelously, and Junior could feel her mild, professional satisfaction as she prepared to complete the exchange.

"And what are we supposed to do with these materials?"

"Try not to kill yourselves. And share." Senior turned back to their vessel.

Junior felt uneasy. Everything had gone so smoothly. Exactly as expected. Senior's delivery was flawless. So what was worrying her? Before she turned to follow Senior, she noticed a group of mostly young humans standing nearby. Their skin was darker than that of the Security Council members, though not darker than some of the armored guards. The group held signs painted with bold, red letters:

UNITED NATIONS, DIVIDED PEOPLE

NO ONE ASKED FOR YOUR "HELP"

LOCAL > GLOBAL

Junior turned to the protesters. She knew what she was about to do was a serious breach of protocol. She would be reprimanded. Maybe even removed from her esteemed role as a diplomat. And more importantly, she would undercut Senior's authority, disrespecting her very first mentor at the worst possible time. But she heard her words before she could stop them.

She asked, "We have heard from one human. What do *you* say?"

The group's members started in surprise. They had not expected to be acknowledged by the United Nations, let alone a delegation from another planet. The smallest one stepped forward.

"I say this deal sounds a lot like the deals my grandparents made."

The president whipped his reddened face from the group to Junior and interjected quickly through his sound amplifier. "Yes, well... youthful spirit but no tact, as you can see. Thank you for your promise of gifts. Rest assured, they will be received graciously."

Senior observed the unexpected interaction. To Junior's immense relief, she did not scold or interfere. Perhaps she knew this diatribe would only cement their efforts here. Or perhaps she just welcomed the break in routine after such a long career. Neither Shepherd responded to the president.

Junior continued questioning the child. "What deal did your grandparents make?"

"They gave up freedoms they didn't know they could lose. To fight wars they didn't start."

"What freedoms?"

An older protester added her voice. "There is only one freedom. To be us, not them, not you."

"We do not ask you to be us. We only invite you to grow. To join us in the stars when you are ready."

"You ask us to trade our technologies and conflicts for yours. To grow as though we do not already know how. *Some* of us know how, at least. It amounts to the same thing."

Junior did not know what to say. She felt a flush of embarrassment, followed by consternation. It certainly did not amount to the same thing. Even with gifts of highly advanced technology, it would be generations before humans could aid the Shepherds in any meaningful way. And even then, the humans would not grow to three times their current size, sprouting new legs and sense organs in the process. They would still be human. And besides, they would die without help. That inevitability was made plain by their leadership. What did *some of us* mean?

In the silence of Junior's perplexity and the rising chatter, Senior addressed the now massive crowd encircling the visitors, panning her head from left to right to show she meant all to hear. "Perhaps these young ones should represent you. They are wise to choose their destiny with care. You do not know us. You need not join us. We will share our knowledge as promised. How you use it is your choice. Thank you for this audience."

She bowed her head a final time, and when she turned to their vessel this time, Junior followed. The young Shepherd burned with shame as they lifted through the atmosphere and set in their travel coordinates. When Senior extended a sense tendril, Junior almost refused to take it. But that would be unforgivably rude, and Senior had done nothing to deserve it. The shame was Junior's. She let the veteran diplomat feel it openly.

To her horror, Senior laughed. Before Junior could recoil her tendril, however, she felt the feelings behind the laughter. Tenderness, not mockery.

"You did well today."

"Well? Please do not patronize me. I embarrassed myself. I embarrassed you. I nearly ruined the entire mission."

Senior laughed again. "You worry. That is good. It shows you care about your work. But consider. Would the Academy send a brand-new Shepherd to change the course of an entire species—an entire planet—if they expected perfection?"

"Perhaps not." Junior was mollified somewhat, but still embarrassed. And confused. "But are you not concerned that the humans will not join us after my foolish words?"

"No."

"Why not?"

"Life seeks life. It is one of two fundamental laws of the universe. Maybe the humans will destroy themselves before our gifts arrive. Maybe after. But if they do not, they will seek us out. It is not a choice, but a certainty. We are all they know beyond their world. Once adrift for a time, they will begin to feel alone. No one wants to be alone."

"But..." Junior did not know if she should say this. She did not even know how, the thought still floating, half-formed, in her mind. "The protesters *did* want to be alone. They did not want our gifts. They did not want to join us."

"No one wants to be alone," Senior repeated. "Had the culture of the protesters not been conquered by the culture of the United Nations, we would not have come. All life seeks community. But not all cultures confuse community with colonization."

Junior knew the word of course. Human history was rife

with it. But she and Senior had just changed that history. Everything the humans believed now had to be understood within the context of the Shepherds and their unfathomably advanced technology. But this mission. Her career. Her people. She was aghast. This is not what she signed up for when she applied to the Academy. She probed tentatively, taking time to find the right question. "*Senior*... are we colonizers?"

Senior's tone changed from warmth to something darker. Sadder. "The second fundamental law. As immutable as the first, and only seemingly opposed. The universe craves diversity. Of the countless lifeforms she creates, not one has ever been identical to another. But despite her designs, in our loneliness, we cannot help changing to be more like others. We cannot help insisting others change to be more like us. In the great cycle, we destroy the diversity she creates. It is beyond our control. All we can attempt to control is *how* we change."

"Unless we choose community over colonization, you mean. Unless we refuse the stars." Junior did not know what emotions Senior was sensing through their enfolded tendrils, reeling as she was from her own revelations.

If Senior was as conflicted, she did not let it show. "In my experience, and the experience of countless civilizations, the stars are not so easily ignored." She paused for a long time before continuing. "But perhaps if we do not answer every call, we may remember to hear as those young protesters do." The older diplomat transmitted a swell of pride to her protege. "As you do."

The Shepherds were silent then, letting their senses flow into the infinite darkness beyond their small vessel. There was no hurry. Earth was only the first stop on their way home.

* * *

Discussion Questions

1. Do you believe the aliens are colonizers? How do you differentiate between colonization and widening a community?

2. The protestor says, "They gave up freedoms they didn't know they could lose. To fight wars they didn't start." Is giving up freedom to fight wars you didn't start the natural progression of growing your community to include new cultures?

3. The story has some parallels to European interactions with native communities in the Americas. How are the alien interactions different, and how are they the same? How might the outcomes be different and the same?

4. Senior says (1) "the stars are not so easily ignored" (2) "life seeks life" and (3) "nobody wants to be alone." This suggests that all sentient creatures will naturally attempt to reach the stars. Do you agree or disagree? What evidence do you have to support your opinion?

5. If the humans accept the alien gifts, is the framework for their future irrevocably set? Is there a way to accept the gifts of advanced technology without the gifts forcing their future path?

* * *

They Got Their Show

Garrett Davis

* * *

<u>**Content Disclosure**</u>: Mild Language

* * *

It is midnight in Ponderosa and Nick Velasquez can't sleep. The public doesn't want him to sleep. It's been like this ever since it hit all the big streaming platforms. The viewers stay up bingeing and he... well, he has been bingeing in his own way. With a bottle of tequila in one hand and a lit joint in the other, Nick wanders from room to room like a ghost in his own house. He shuffles through indents made in the living room carpet. Depressions from the furniture his *esposa*, Marcella, took with her when she left. *Can't look at my eyes without seeing our little girl.* Nick pulls on the joint, its coal shifting from a deep cherry red to bright yellow in the darkness. He exhales a plume of smoke and walks down the hall, his sobriety trailing behind him. *And just when things were getting back to normal.* He'd gotten a job at a local taxi company, found a support group with minimal *woo-woo*, hell he'd even gotten Marcella on the phone once or twice, but then the docuseries hit Netflix.

He's been circling the house all evening, like water going down the drain, each revolution getting smaller and smaller bringing him down inevitably to a single point. His daughter's room. Everything is, more or less, as Carmen left it: Notorious B.I.G. posters, a half-made bed, and her diary open to a blank page dated June 17, 1995. Stumbling into the room, he squares off with the closet. A four-year-old Carmen wouldn't sleep if the closet door was left open at night. She got scared that if it were left open, monsters from the dark could just walk on in. So being a good daddy, Nick made a big show of closing the doors and threatening any would-be monsters inside. It became a nightly ritual until at fifteen, her embarrassed protests hit home. Nick takes a swig from the bottle and wipes his mouth using the back of his hand. He'd asked her once why the monsters didn't simply push the door open.

"Daddy," she had said, "the handle is on the outside."

Swaying slightly, it seems to Nick that the evil behind those bifold closet doors is almost palpable. It might be the drugs or maybe it's the liquor, but he swears he can feel pressure built up behind those doors. He sees darkness leaking out from underneath and marvels at the strength of those flimsy tarnished brass hinges. Putting the bottle down, he extends a shaking hand.

"Don't do this," he whispers to himself.

The doors open, revealing stacks upon stacks of banker's boxes. They're piled floor to ceiling, each one labeled in fat black ink: **1995**. He takes a shot of tequila for each box he brings to the living room. Marcella had been nice enough to leave him an old reclining chair and he had since bought a secondhand television. So bathed in blue TV light, Nick gets to work. He organizes statements, arranges and rearranges glossy eight-by-ten photographs. and rereads old newspaper clippings. Back in 1995, Carmen and a local boy Benjie left the house to rent a movie from Blockbuster. They did this every weekend. Nick would give Carmen twenty dollars, and she and Benjie would walk the three blocks to the video store. But on June 17, 1995, they never returned.

The docuseries plays in the background. *When did I put that on?* It details what they call *shady police work* and *circumstantial evidence.* It claims the country has put an innocent man on death row. Nick glances at his masterpiece, laid out just as he remembers it; each document linked by a thread of red string, and they all lead to Benjie. He'd cut Benjie's photo out of one of Carmen's old yearbooks; they'd gone to school together. Benjie is fat in the photo, his face pitted with acne. Every grad class has one fat loser that no one likes—no one but Carmen that is. Nick puffs on his joint in contemplation. He never understood what made them such fast friends. He finds his answer in another memory, something Marcella once told him. Her words hang in the forefront of his mind and he's so high he swears he can actually hear her say it.

"She wants to fix him," Marcella had said. "She just doesn't know that yet."

"Well, she's certainly not in it for his brains," Nick says aloud, reliving the conversation in real time. "If I had a lineup of potential school shooters... I'd pick that sad little *puto* nine out of ten times."

The public, however, didn't seem to feel that way. Benjie is on the screen now, much older and less ruddy in the face. Nick suspects he's wearing makeup for the shot. The lighting is good—the angle flattering—he almost looks handsome. *Like lipstick on a pig.*

"Did you kill Carmen Velasquez?" the interviewer asks.

"No," Benjie answers. "Why, uh, why's everyone still asking that? I've been in here nearly, uh, twenty years and my story hasn't changed. And do you want to know why?"

"Why?" the reporter asks.

"'Cause it's the truth. I ain't never hurt a fly in my life."

When Benjie says this, Nick hears the pings: likes and retweets being sent out from the viewers. He picks them up like radio waves on teeth fillings. They sound like the bells and whistles on an old pinball machine. *I'm on a whole 'nother frequency, hombre!* That's when it falls apart. He sees the mistake in his careful plotting on the floor.

Benjie and Carmen were found three blocks from the Blockbuster video in an alley. Benjie was unconscious and Carmen... both of them were covered in her blood. The autopsy report says her throat had been slit from behind, but that the cut hadn't been deep enough to be fatal. The attacker—probably in a panic—had bludgeoned her to death with a cinderblock that had been used as a doorstop. The knife was in Benjie's unconscious hand when the police arrived. Benjie never denied the knife was his. His toxicology came back clean. There was nothing to explain his blackout. The detail that Nick had overlooked all this time was the pendant of St. Christopher hanging around Carmen's neck. The patron saint of protection, a birthday gift in case Daddy wasn't around to deal with the monsters. It is missing in the crime scene photo. Benjie had been searched and it wasn't on his person at the time. Nor could it be found in the subsequent combing of the crime scene. *Could someone else have taken it? Would that prove someone else was there?*

A phone rings, yanking Nick from his thoughts and making him jump. The call display says: Dispatch. Everyone in the company is required to be on call once a week. That means if some suit and tie needs a lift to the airport at three a.m. you saddle up and ride. Tonight isn't his night, he's sure of it, and so he lets it go to voicemail. The display goes dark momentarily before dancing and lighting up again. Nick picks up, opening his mouth to set free a string of expletives only to find his brain hadn't yet finished translating them to English. What does come out is a sort of involuntary muffled burp.

"Listen Nicky, before you fly off the handle," the dispatcher says, "I want you to know that I know it's late. Not only that," he continues, "but I know it's not your night tonight. I got a call you might find interesting."

There's a beeping as Dispatch patches two lines together. When it's done, Nick hears a recording taken for quality assurance purposes. The recording starts with an automated message from the incoming caller. It says:

"You have a collect call from Ponderosa Penitentiary. To accept charges and connect, please press the pound key." A button is pressed and the line crackles as it is transferred.

"Ponderosa Taxi, how may I direct your call?" the recording says.

"Uh, hello?" comes an unmistakable voice from the other side. "I was wondering if I, uh, could schedule a pickup?"

Suddenly, it feels hard to breathe. Nick's throat feels as though he's been gargling gravel and sleet. He knows that voice, has heard that voice in his haunted dreams for nearly thirty years—Benjie.

"What's the address?" asks Dispatch.

"Well, uh, I get out tomorrow and I—will you pick people up from the prison or is that weird?"

"We'll pick you up but we won't break you out."

Benjie laughs. The thought of anything resembling joy coming from his piggy snout makes Nick's blood boil. He almost hangs up right then and there, he wants to throw the phone and watch the cheap plastic explode into a million little pieces, but he doesn't. Instead, he snuffs out the joint in a crystal ashtray and brings the liquor bottle to his lips. Nothing comes out. The worm clinks against the bottleneck.

"Nicky? Are you still there?"

"Yeah," Nick says. "I'm here."

"So, what do you say?"

"I say you got some goddamn giant bull balls. Did you dream this up on your own? Who put this *loca* idea into your thick skull?"

"Whoa, Nick buddy," he replies. "I don't know what you think I'm suggesting, but whatever it is, I ain't! I just figured that maybe you'd want to see him. Maybe apologize, get that—uh, whatcha call it—document?"

Nick sits down in his recliner. His head hurts something fierce. Pinching the bridge of his nose, he says, "It's denouement, not document, a nice neat ending."

"Well, well, well... look at the big brain on you! Listen, his gran passed away while he's been locked up. Give him a lift to her old house. Get whatever is on your chest out and in the open, and say your goodbyes. Hell, he'll probably skip town after! I know I would. The whole world knowing my story... I'd get out."

Nick stares at the pictures lined up on the floor; all the papers, the bits of string. Reminders of his sobriety going up in smoke. These snapshots are all that he has left of his daughter. It'd been hard to let her go, even knowing that the man responsible was behind bars... what would he do now? "I'll think about it," he says.

"You'll do the right thing," Dispatch replies. "See you tomorrow."

There's a click and the line goes dead. Nick jumps to his feet and launches the phone at the television. Spiderweb-like fissures bloom from the impact crater. The pixels fail to communicate with each other, and the colors go all wrong. A large triangular swath of the screen goes lime green. The footage cuts to Benjie at a metal picnic table in the prison's exercise yard. He's looking wistfully out through the fence to the hills beyond. A yellow shard splits his sitting area in two. The sky is red with color distortion. Someone from behind the camera asks, "Do you think if Carmen were around today, you'd still be friends?"

"Uh, oh yeah," Benjie says. "Even now."

The episode ends. The credits roll, and Nick passes out.

The next morning has Nick's head feeling like an egg about to hatch. He opens bloodshot eyes to find himself lying on the floor amidst his papers. He doesn't remember hauling the banker's boxes out. He kisses his finger and plants it on a photo of Carmen. *What am I going to do?* Bones creak as he pulls himself up to his feet. His saliva is thick and acrid tasting from last night's binge, so he lumbers over to the kitchen and puts his head under the faucet. Cool water runs across his face, soothing the pounding heat within his head. Then when the water clears of rust, he takes a mouthful, gargles, and spits it back into the sink. He's drying himself with a hand towel when the phone goes off again. This time it's only his alarm: nine thirty. The television screen is still on—still fractured—and stuck on a pause menu.

It asks him: Are you still there?

He runs a hand over his shaved scalp. *Am I all here? Would I know if I wasn't?* He vaguely remembers talking to Dispatch on the phone but is unsure what had driven him to pick up in the middle of the night. Regardless, the *pendejo* Benjie is getting out today and Nick wants to be there... for better or worse.

Ponderosa's prison is surrounded by artificial hills made of red sand. These mounds make it so the entire complex sits in a gulley. Towers are situated at each corner of the high fence line and are made of gray concrete and tan brick. Local legend has it that an inmate tried to escape once. He allegedly managed to get through the fence but was shot through the head by an eagle-eyed sniper in the furthest tower. A camera crew is set up at the front gate, awaiting thirty-six-year-old Benjie to set foot outside the penitentiary for the first time in twenty years.

The road is surprisingly crowded for being so far outside the city limits. Nick parks his taxi on the shoulder across the street. A crowd of onlookers, fans of the series, watch and wait for Benjie along with the local news crew. Nick pulls a ball cap down low on his head and gets out of the vehicle in order to mingle with the crowd.

It isn't long before a lone figure in ill-fitting khakis and a faded jean jacket makes his way down the long-fenced corridor toward freedom. Prison food and weights had robbed Benjie of his girth and transformed him into a short lean man. Although the ruddy red cheeks remain. Nick shivers despite the asphalt radiating midday heat, baking him from below. The hairs on the back of his neck stand up. It's more like seeing a zombie than a ghost—a recognizable face and body, but devoid of the soul.

For years Nick had prepared to watch this man die, had dreamed of being there when the needle plunger was pushed. He tries to summon some of that rage, that kind that made him wish old sparky hadn't been outlawed. The kind of rage that makes eye for an eye seem reasonable. He finds that he can't. *Maybe Benjie is a victim of the docuseries as well.* Could the true villain be the corporation? Is it right to profit off the pain of grieving families? Parading corpses like science projects to pick apart; as if justice is no longer about right and wrong, but about who can argue their points best. Just how could they have eight one-hour-long episodes, interviewing every relation and suspect about how they knew Carmen and not uncover who she was? How she would sing in the shower till there was no hot water left in the house or how she was such a fussy eater she'd eat French fries but not a baked potato. *That her first words had been Dada.*

No one was here for Carmen; they were all here for Benjie. The crowd of onlookers rise from their lawn chairs and cheer. Some of the tailgaters shake up beer cans and open them, spraying foam everywhere. Women wave hand-painted signs with hashtags like: **#WESTANDWITHBENJIE, #INNOCENTUNTILPROVENGUILTY, #MISSINGNECKLACE.**

Benjie sees them, too, but quickly looks to the ground, his cheeks getting redder still. Then without looking up, he raises a fist into the air and the onlookers go wild. It sounds like the home team had just won the Super Bowl outside the prison.

A correctional officer stops Benjie at the gate. They exchange a few words, smile, and shake hands. The guard opens the door and the inmate steps through a free man. More cheering. Someone lights off a few bottle rockets that go whistling overhead, their pops unheard amidst the jubilation. Microphones are held in front of Benjie's face.

"Benjie," says one reporter, "tell us how you feel."

"Uh," Benjie scratches the stubble under his chin. "I guess I'm glad it's over."

"Benjie," another says, "what's the first thing you'll do now that you're out?"

"Oh, I've been thinking about this one a lot," he answers. "I'm going to finally rent *Toy Story* from Blockbuster."

The reporters, crew, and crowd all chuckle at this. No one is thinking of Carmen. Why should they? The public's hive mind has a short memory. They don't care much for the dead and gone. Benjie is alive; he might still have a future. Everyone likes a happy ending, don't they?

"Benjie, do you have anything to say to the family of Carmen Velasquez?"

After a pause, Benjie slowly replies, "You have no idea how sad I've been. Uh, thinking about how this series shows that, well, that the guy that killed Carmen is still out there. And well, that just makes it all fresh again, don't it? I understand how badly they wanted justice, and uh, I just want them to know that I don't blame them for that."

No more than ten yards away, hidden amidst the throng of people, Nick clenches his jaw and nods absently as Benjie speaks. His old man had the same expression on his face when his mother passed. He hadn't understood it at the time, but he understands it now. It's the look of a strong man trying his best not to break. He wants to call out to Benjie to... to apologize. To fight. Let them have it out right there in front of the cameras. And after, maybe then Nick could cry. He opens his mouth once, twice, three times—but nothing comes out.

Shoulders slumping, he wants nothing more than to sit down or shower. He feels... dirty. He retires to the taxicab and cranks the AC to max, content, watching the rest from afar. Benjie shakes hands with his supporters, one of the tailgaters offers him a cold beer and he drinks it. His lips pucker at the taste and everyone laughs yet again. It strikes Nick just then that will have been Benjie's first legal drink. *Imagine, your first beer at thirty-six!*

When things begin to wind down, Nick flicks on the taxi's service light. Benjie shakes one last hand and clambers into the back seat. Nick starts the car, and Benjie rattles off his grandmother's address. Benjie is flustered by all the activity. From the rearview mirror, Nick can make out the dopey half grin he's wearing. Nick starts the car and the locks click shut. With the hat and glasses Benjie hasn't recognized him.

"Gee," Benjie says after a few miles in silence, "I forgot how fast cars are. I remember, uh, that I used to get carsick. If I get carsick, will you pull over?"

Benjie's knuckles are white on the armrests.

"Sure, Benjie," Nick mumbles and his knuckles are white on the steering wheel.

"Say, uh, I didn't give you my name. Did you watch the series?"

"Something like that," Nick says, taking off the glasses.

Even so, it takes Benjie a minute to realize who is in the

front seat. *Christ, have I aged that much or is the* pendejo *slower than I remember?*

"Mr.-Mr. Velasquez?" Benjie blinks rapidly. "What are you doing here?"

"You've been in for a long time Benjie, I work for the cab company now."

"I guess a lot has changed, huh?" Benjie sits back in his seat, relaxing ever so slightly.

"Everything has changed," Nick agrees, "and nothing. Carmen is still gone. Did you know, I got your parole denied? You were sixteen years old when Carmen was killed. You should have got parole after ten years. Does that piss you off?"

"I mean, yeah," Benjie says with a shrug. "But I had a long time to uh think, I mean while I was inside. At first, I felt like you were killing me, you know? Taking my best years, but then I thought-I thought you know, I'd probably do the same if our positions were reversed."

"Why did you do it Benjie?"

"I didn't, Mr. Velasquez, I swear."

"I mean the docuseries?" Nick says.

"I'm innocent," Benjie says, "and it really helped that other fella, uh, a state over clear his name. It meant freedom. You don't know what it's like being called a murderer for twenty years when you and, uh, God know that you didn't do nothing."

"You know what it meant to me?" Nick says, watching Benjie shake his head no in the rearview. "It meant that Carmen had to die all over again. Twenty years of people raising her from the dead, digging through the wreckage of my life, and for what? To help you? I was convinced you did it. Convinced that you took my sweet daughter away from me."

"And, uh what do you think now, uh, sir?"

"I don't even know anymore," Nick sighs. "Seems to me all these networks want to glorify murder and mystery, and in the end, it don't matter if you did it or not. If you did kill Carmen they got their show, and if you didn't... well, they still got their show. Doesn't seem right to me and I'm just caught in the thresher."

The silence weighs heavy between them as they drive due south down the highway. The exit to Benjie's grandmother's house is a mile off. Tumbleweeds roll past in the opposite lane and get swept up in the swirls of dust left by the taxicab as it blows past.

"You know," Benjie says, his face going red, "I loved her too. But I, uh, don't think she liked me that way, you know?"

"Have you ever blacked out before, Benjie?"

"No," Benjie admits. "That was the first time. Could you uh, slow down, Mr. Velasquez? I'm feeling ill."

The taxi goes past the exit, leaving Ponderosa behind.

Benjie's brow furrows. "Say, uh, where are we going?"

"We're going to Blockbuster, buddy," Nick says. "I'm taking you to Blockbuster."

* * *

This story is a part of our legacy-of-excellence program, first printed in the After Dinner Conversation—August 2021 issue.

Discussion Questions

1. If there was a Netflix-style docuseries about the person accused of killing your loved one, would you watch it?

2. Do you think Nick will have peace now? If so, what is causing him to have that peace, and why didn't he have it sooner?

3. Does it matter if Benjie is really innocent or guilty? Do your feelings about the story, or the decisions/changes in the characters, change if Benjie secretly is the killer?

4. Is it fair that a Netflix investigation series helped prove Benjie's innocence and get him out of jail? Does it matter that there may be other innocent people who weren't lucky enough to get their own Netflix special?

5. What would you have done (*or said*) if you had been Nick, driving the taxi, in the story?

* * *

Author Information

The Apath

A.J. Parker grew up in Phoenix, Arizona, then spent some time on the East Coast trying to make up for all that water she lost. She's a digital journalist by day and a writer by night. Her poems have been published in ten literary journals, including *Feminist Food Journal* and *Ink in Thirds*. Instagram, Threads, X (Twitter), and Bluesky *@authorajparker*; Substack *@updateswithaj.substack.com*

Specter

Alexis Ames is a speculative fiction writer with works in publications such as *Pseudopod, Luna Station Quarterly,* and *Radon Journal.*
X (Twitter) *@alexis_writes1; www.alexisamesbooks.com*

One Out of Four

Joseph S. Klapach is an attorney who lives in Los Angeles with his wife and children. The only thing he loves more than a good dinner is a good conversation.

Face Chopping

J.S. McQueen is a Colorado paralegal and ex-educator. She writes science fiction and fantasy with elements of romance and horror.
X (Twitter) *@JSNicShuibhne;* Bluesky *@jsmcqueen.bsky.social*

Freeing Free Will

Matthew Thomas Bernell is an emerging writer from the Midwest. He holds degrees in Spanish, English, and philosophy from Purdue University. Recently, his work has appeared in the journals *North American Review*, *New Ohio Review*, *The Pinch*, and *Chestnut Review*.
X (Twitter) *@ImmanentFlux*

Shepherds

Aweed Nyoka, after a decade of playing soldier, fell in love with an artist and discovered creating feels better than the other thing. His speculative fiction asks serious questions of surprising subjects, from rabbinical felines to murderous fungi. He has published decidedly non-speculative poetry in *Tendon Magazine* and writes a new story for his son every week.

They Got Their Show

Garrett Davis is a plumber by day and a writer whenever he can muster the courage. He lives in B.C.

Additional Information

Reviews

If you enjoyed reading these stories, please consider doing an online review. It's only a few seconds of your time, but it is very important in continuing the series. Good reviews mean higher rankings. Higher rankings mean more sales and a greater ability to release stories.

Print Books

https://www.afterdinnerconversation.com

Purchase our growing collection of print anthologies, "Best of," and themed print book collections. Available from our website, online bookstores, and by order from your local bookstore.

Podcast Discussions/Audiobooks

https://www.afterdinnerconversation.com/podcastlinks

Listen to our podcast discussions and audiobooks of After Dinner Conversation short stories on Apple, Spotify, or wherever podcasts are played. Or, if you prefer, watch the podcasts on our YouTube channel or download the .mp3 file directly from our website.

Patreon

https://www.patreon.com/afterdinnerconversation

Get early access to short stories and ad-free podcasts. New supporters also get a free digital copy of the anthology *After Dinner Conversation— Season One*. Support us on Patreon!

Book Clubs/Classrooms

https://www.afterdinnerconversation.com/book-club-downloads

After Dinner Conversation supports book clubs! Receive free short stories for your book club to read and discuss!

Social

Connect with us on Facebook, YouTube, Instagram, Bluesky, TikTok, Substack, and Twitter.

Special Thanks

After Dinner Conversation gratefully acknowledges the support of the following individuals and organizations.

* * *

In Alphabetical Order

Anonymous, Marie Anderson, DB Babak, Ria Bruns, Brett Clark, Jarvis Coffin, Rebecca Dueben, Tina Forsee, Deb Gain-Braley, David Gibson, Mercedes Holmes, Ron Koch, Sandra Kolankiewicz, Donna Lormand, Rena Ong, Anja Peerdeman, John Sheirer, David Shultz, Frank Strada, Mitchell Sweet, Annie Thompson, and Bill Weston.

After Dinner Conversation is supported in part by the Arizona Commission on the Arts, which receives support from the State of Arizona and the National Endowment for the Arts.

* * *

Donation Information

Please send your 501(c)(3) donations to:
After Dinner Conversation
2516 S. Jentilly Lane, Tempe, AZ 85282
https://www.afterdinnerconversation.com/donation
https://www.patreon.com/afterdinnerconversation

Made in United States
Cleveland, OH
16 February 2025

14407008R00073